Surviving an Eating Disorder

Surviving an Eating Disorder

Strategies for Family and Friends

THIRD EDITION · *Revised and Updated*

MICHELE SIEGEL, Ph.D.

JUDITH BRISMAN, Ph.D.

MARGOT WEINSHEL, M.S.W.

HARPER

NEW YORK · LONDON · TORONTO · SYDNEY

This book is designed to give information on various medical conditions, treatments and procedures for your personal knowledge and to help you be a more informed consumer of medical and health services. It is not intended to be complete or exhaustive, nor is it a substitute for the advice of your physician. You should seek medical care promptly for any specific medical condition or problem you may have.

All efforts have been made to ensure the accuracy of the information contained in this book as of the date published. The authors and the publisher expressly disclaim responsibility for any adverse effects arising from the use or application of the information contained herein.

SURVIVING AN EATING DISORDER. Copyright © 1988, 1997, 2009 by Judith Brisman, Margot Weinshel, and the estate of Michele Siegel. All rights reserved. Printed in the United States of America. No part of this book may be used or reproduced in any manner whatsoever without written permission except in the case of brief quotations embodied in critical articles and review. For information, address HarperCollins Publishers, 10 East 53rd Street, New York, NY 10022.

HarperCollins books may be purchased for educational, business, or sales promotional use. For information please write: Special Markets Department, HarperCollins Publishers, 10 East 53rd Street, New York, NY 10022.

First Collins Living edition published 2009

Designed by Ashley Halsey

Library of Congress Cataloging-in-Publication Data
Siegel, Michele.
    Surviving an eating disorder : strategies for family and friends / Michele Siegel, Judith Brisman, Margot Weinshel. — 3rd ed., rev. and updated.
        p. cm.
    Includes index.
    ISBN 978-0-06-169895-8
1. Eating disorders—Patients—Family relationships. I. Brisman, Judith. II. Weinshel, Margot. III. Title.
    RC552.E18S54 2009
    616.85'2606–dc22

2008047450

*To our patients and their families, who, in their
willingness to share their struggles, have asked us
the questions and taught us the answers.*

Contents

Acknowledgments

One can only hope that it is possible to change the world by virtue of having lived a life. Michele Siegel lived a life filled with joy, spirit, and a laughter that embraced all around her. She also knew that the families we treated had been somehow lost in the mix, and she worked hard to change that. *Surviving an Eating Disorder* was Michele's idea, and for each family supported by this book, we want to acknowledge Michele for her inspiration from the start.

Frances Goldin, our agent, changes the world daily with an ever-present sense of dignity, fight, and quiet persistence (sometimes not so quiet!). She fought for this book's stability and in that sense allowed *Surviving* to come alive. Changes in any reader's life as a result of this book are in no small part thanks to her.

Our editor, Anne Cole, has been a steady and supportive force throughout, knowing that just a nuanced shift in direction can allow for a completely new route to travel. Melainie Rogers contributed her knowledge about nutrition with intelligence and clarity, in the very way she does when she works collaboratively with patients in treatment. Rebecca Johnson nearly sacrificed her holiday vacation to research the details of this book. She has helped to seamlessly pick up the pieces in many different arenas. We are very grateful. And the therapists at the Eating Disorder Resource Center in Manhattan are a mainstay source of support and intellectual challenge.

Julia and Senna Lauer cannot be thanked enough for their laughter and love and for teaching more than any training program could possibly allow. They provide the joy and richness of life that is an ongoing beacon guiding the way home.

Acknowledgments

Thanks to Robert, Rebecca, and Josh Bazell for their help in the original writing of this book. Stephanie Bazell was born when the first edition of *Surviving* was published. She, too, is 20 years old. Her support, knowledge, and humor during the writing of the revisions have been a great source of inspiration.

Finally, we thank our patients and their families for letting us know what works—and what doesn't. Without their voices, this book would be without truth and soul. Their words and experiences remind us always of what we need to know next.

Introduction

How to Survive

Another 10 years have passed since the last revision of *Surviving an Eating Disorder*. Lives have changed; children have been born; life sometimes joyfully, sometimes relentlessly, moves forward. Memories of Michele Siegel, who died in 1993, have been woven into our souls. It was Michele's thinking, ideas, and humor that helped carry *Surviving* through its initial writing. Her words, sensibilities, and advice remain an integral part of the book.

Now interwoven into our lives are also the lives of our children. Our roles as parents have grown and shifted over these last years. Margot has shepherded her grown children into the world. Judith's daughters, who were only a thought during previous writings, are now richly embedded in her day-to-day life. The ever challenging and changing roles as parents have no doubt allowed us to speak to parents from within the trenches. We both know how fulfilling—and complicated—parenting can be. We know from experience that there is never one solution to a problem, and the second you think you know what you are doing, something changes, and you're proven completely wrong. We come to this writing informed not just with new information but, perhaps more importantly, with new life experience.

Indeed, not only have we changed, but the culture has changed as well. Insurance informs how many treatments evolve. Shorter term inpatient stays are the norm now, so we have had to creatively consider what else can allow for a higher level of care when it is needed. The question now often is not if medication is needed, but which medication will best help. Intensive outpatient programs are often an ongoing part of the treatment experience.

As treatment options change, the role of parents changes as well. An intensive intervention to help parents refeed their anorexic child (the Maudsley approach) has nudged parents to the center of the treatment arena. Parents have been urged to take charge of their children's eating and weight patterns and have been encouraged to play a more dominant role in the daily care of a child in trouble.

For some parents, however, involvement has been, at best, problematic. Here, interventions only exacerbate issues of intrusion and authoritative control. For others, refeeding helps at some points and results in crises at others. Questions remain: How can someone with an eating disorder best be supported in taking control of her own life? How can she battle behaviors that leave her victim to her own feelings or the needs and desires of others?

This latest edition of *Surviving an Eating Disorder* has been written to address the changes that have occurred since the first and second editions of this book. We have revisited the bedrock of our thinking— that is, we want to understand what helps someone become responsible for her own life—and we have integrated new information and research to consider what roles will best help the person with the eating disorder as well as anyone involved.

This book is written for all of you who are living with or in a relationship with someone who has an eating problem. Perhaps you are a parent, spouse, or sibling of the person with the problem. You may be a lover, roommate, colleague, or friend. You may already know that a disorder exists because signs of the problem are obvious, or a doctor or therapist may have diagnosed it. Or you may be aware of peculiar eating and/or weight problems but not know if a serious disorder is present. The person you know may or may not already be involved in some kind of treatment. As readers, you come to this book from a wide range of experiences with the sufferer.

Yours is a difficult position to be in. You want to help, but you're not sure what is best. You may be witness to many behaviors that are destructive and frightening, as well as disruptive to a household or a relationship. Not knowing what to do can make you feel helpless and confused.

To add to the confusion, the guidance you receive from professionals may completely contradict itself. Some professionals tell you to get in there and take control of the eating. Others tell you that any attempt to stop the disordered eating will result in a control battle that will only make the problem worse. With no clear-cut line of approach, you may be more confused than ever.

Because you are not the one with the actual problem, however, your own difficulties may be overlooked. *Your* suffering and confusion about how to proceed may very well go unnoticed or untreated. People in your position can easily become the silent sufferers—the unseen victims of the eating disorder.

This book is written for you. We know how hard it is at home—and we know that you may not know what to do next. We will talk to you about how to consider the goals given your own particular situation. We will discuss what you can do to help and what you can expect from the eating-disordered person—and yourself.

This book is about recovery—not only that of the eating-disordered person, but of your recovery and the recovery of your relationship as well.

Surviving an Eating Disorder can be used as a general reference book to pick up whenever you are faced with the question "What do I do now?" However, this is not just a guidebook. *Surviving an Eating Disorder* examines eating problems with the goal of broadening your perspective on the difficulties you see and furthering your understanding of the complex syndromes of anorexia nervosa, bulimia nervosa, and binge-eating disorder. The combination of perspectives and strategies offered in this book can provide you with a new and richer awareness of both the eating disorder and your relationship with the person about whom you are concerned.

The first-person stories and case examples in this book accurately reflect the feelings, experiences, and circumstances expressed by patients, their families, and friends, but all names, locales, and identifying details have been changed.

Part I

Gaining Perspective

1

What You See

The Behavioral Aspects of Eating Disorders

I looked over at my 11-year-old daughter, Lara, as the internist spoke to us. "Anorexic. Your daughter is anorexic," the doctor said. I watched Lara cross her sticklike arms in reaction to these words. Her face suddenly looked old to me, bony, unpleasantly pointed. My heart sank. How could I not have noticed how much weight she had lost? Things had been going so well. She was a straight-A student. She never seemed like she had any problems on her mind. When had I stopped noticing?

Barbara L., 39-year-old mother

I came home early from work with flowers, thinking I'd surprise my wife. When I put the key in the door, I was met with a frantic cry, "Wait! Who is it? Ben? Don't come in yet! Wait!" I panicked—I thought the worst and raced into the apartment. And there was Nina, standing in the middle of the kitchen. Several boxes of cakes, cookies, and a pie were opened and half eaten. Candy wrappers were strewn over the floor. The refrigerator door hung wide open. A puddle of spilt milk rested in the middle of the table; ice cream was melting in the container beside it. Nina looked at me angrily. "Why didn't you call?" she demanded. "Why are you home so early?" A moment before I had been so sure I would find her with another man—but this? This didn't make any sense to me—in a frightening way, it felt worse. What had I walked in on? What was happening to my wife? I remember not knowing what to do with the flowers.

Ben, 27-year-old husband

It's getting harder and harder living with Jennie. It's almost like living with two different people. Half the time she is on some diet or other, following it to the T, not an inch of leeway. Then suddenly she's eating like a mad-woman, and it's possible that at any time all the food in the house can disappear. During these times she won't go out, she'll break plans with me, and she will look miserable and depressed. All she wants to talk about is what she's eaten, how "good" she's been, or how different life will be at a low weight. She could stand to lose weight—she's about 180 pounds. But even when she does get thinner, which happens periodically, it seems that starts the whole cycle over again. Jennie's my best friend, but I've had enough. Is there something I can do?

Pamela, 24-year-old roommate

When Eating Habits Become Eating Disorders

The mother, husband, and friend in the above examples knew that something was wrong. What they were seeing was not normal behavior.

The people with whom they were involved were in trouble. In all three cases, there were clear signs that the person about whom they cared was eating disordered.

When an eating disorder exists, it is recognized by certain behaviors, the most noticeable being an obsession with food and weight. This obsession can take the form of binge eating, starving, vomiting, compulsive exercising, or other behaviors focused on eating, getting rid of, or avoiding food.

Eating disorders, however, are not merely problems with food. They are psychological disorders, many aspects of which are not apparent to an outside observer.

It is often not easy to tell who is and who is not suffering with an eating disorder. Dieting, exercising, fasting, and a preoccupation with food and weight are so much a part of our culture that it is unusual to find a teenage girl or woman who is not or has not been concerned with weight. It only takes a glance at the covers of women's magazines to see the relentless focus on staying slim. Fashion, advertising, and entertainment idealize a female body that only a small percentage of women can hope to achieve. However, the value of slimness is not the only message these magazines communicate. Alongside the messages to be slim are ads and recipes for rich, enticing desserts. Our culture seems to encourage us all to "have our cake and eat it too."

Almost everyone is susceptible to our culture's messages. Comments like "You look so good. Did you lose weight?" perpetuate the importance of being thin. There are few people who don't enjoy these compliments. In fact, thinness is such a desirable attribute that, in a large study at Harvard University and Radcliffe, it was found that body dissatisfaction and the desire to lose weight are the norm for 70 percent of young women.[1]

It is not just women who are being affected by the culture's messages. Men are also becoming increasingly food and weight conscious. We have only to look at the advertisements, cosmetics, and fitness magazines directed toward men to see that they are no longer excluded from society's emphasis on good looks and slim physique. In fact, men may well be at risk for "reverse" anorexia, in which one sees extreme efforts to increase body size and muscle mass.[2] It seems that no one can escape the message that you just aren't good enough the way you are.

The focus on body image, dieting, and weight is particularly acute among teenagers. Teenage girls are constantly vying to be the thinnest or skipping meals to lose weight. Talking about eating, overeating, and even participating in group "pigouts" are communal experiences. More troubling is the fact that this dissatisfaction with one's body is occurring at ever younger ages. In a recent study, weight concerns and body dissatisfaction were assessed for 182 girls when they were five, seven, and nine years old. The study found that girls as young as age five display significant dissatisfaction with their body.[3] Another study showed that girls as young as three already had a preference for the culture's thin, idealized body type.[4]

Regardless of the age group, it seems that food and weight are on everyone's mind. Does this mean, then, that everyone in our society has an eating disorder? No.

An eating disorder exists when one's attitude toward food and weight has gone awry—when one's feelings about work, school, and relationships, one's day-to-day activities, and one's experience of emotional well-being are determined by what has or has not been eaten or by a number on the scale. Most of us know what it is like to comfort or reward ourselves with food, to allow ourselves an indulgent meal after a particularly difficult day, to have extra calories when we feel disappointed. Most of us know how it feels to wish we looked a little thinner in that bathing suit or to want to look particularly good for an important occasion. However, when these wishes or rewards turn into the basis of all decisions, when the pounds prevent us from going to the beach, when our looks are more important than the occasion itself, then there are indications of a problem deserving attention.

Eating problems usually start out with the common wish to lose weight and maintain a certain body image. These are concerns that most of us have experienced. Often people can go through a period of intensive dieting, obsession with weight, or overeating that will be short-lived and end without outside interventions. However, a potentially short-lived bout with food control becomes an eating disorder when the eating behaviors are no longer used merely to maintain or reduce weight. An eating habit becomes an eating disorder when the primary need it satisfies is psychological, not physical. The eating behavior then becomes a vehicle for the expression of problems outside the arena of calories.

Someone who is eating disordered does not eat because she is physically hungry. She eats for reasons unrelated to physiological needs. That is, the eating may temporarily block out painful feelings, calm anxiety, or subdue tensions. Or the person may starve, not because she is full, but because she wants to control her bodily needs.

Consider Corey's situation for a moment. Corey is a 28-year-old who came to us for help. When Corey was a teenager and became upset because of a school event or a canceled date, she found it comforting to sit in front of the television and slowly savor a piece of chocolate cake or other dessert from her mother's well-stocked kitchen. During this time, she was of normal weight. While she always enjoyed her late-night snacks, they were certainly not the focus of her thinking or plans.

When Corey left home to go to college, however, she began to have more trying times. She felt somewhat overwhelmed by the demands of living on her own in a new environment. Frequently, she felt homesick. More and more often, she looked forward to the late-night snacks (which actually began to occur earlier and earlier in the evening). She found the food soothing, and she could block out her thoughts when she ate. As the school year progressed, Corey found herself thinking about and looking forward to eating as soon as she woke up. Her thoughts started to revolve around what she would eat at mealtimes and what snacks she could buy throughout the day.

She was soon feeling that the rest of her life was secondary to eating. The consequent weight gain accelerated Corey's withdrawal from her social life to a world of food. At this point, Corey could no longer be considered a normally "food-obsessed" teenager; her focus on food, her social withdrawal, and the bingeing were all signs that her eating habits were now part of an eating disorder.

Karla, on the other hand, could be considered to be eating disordered from the early age of 13. As soon as she began to develop physically, Karla recalls, the natural roundness of her shape led her to worry about becoming overweight, and she started to control her food intake and weight. She decided that at five feet, two inches, it was okay to weigh 95 pounds, absolutely no more (and she found it too difficult to weigh less). Since age 13, Karla has remained at 95 pounds. She is now 30 years old. She weighs herself six to ten times daily. If her weight fluctuates at all and rises above 95 pounds, she will do anything possible to make the scale show 95 again. Her efforts include exercising rigorously throughout the day and night (sometimes until 3:00 or 4:00 a.m., when her weight finally returns to 95 pounds), sitting in a sauna wrapped in plastic wrap (to sweat out the liquids), and certainly not eating or drinking anything (including water) until the scale again reaches the magical number 95. If Karla has anything planned for a day when her weight happens to be 96 pounds, she will either cancel the event or know that she will have a bad time. When asked "How can you know you will have a bad time at a party before you get there?" Karla answers simply, "Because I'm 96 pounds and feel fat." Karla's rigid attitude certainly signals the clinical picture of an eating disorder—that is, one's experience of day-to-day situations being rigidly determined by one's weight and food intake.

The Eating Disorders

When people talk about "eating disorders," they are usually referring to either anorexia nervosa, bulimia nervosa, or binge-eating disorder—or some combination of the three. The sections that follow will describe the signs and symptoms characteristic of each disorder.

Checklists are included at the end of this chapter to help you recognize and identify signs of trouble. Your understanding of the disorders will help you confront the problem and get the professional help that is needed. (Further information is provided in Chapters 4 and 6.) The better informed you are about what you see, the better able you will be to discuss your concerns openly, clearly, and in a manner that can be helpful.

Anorexia Nervosa

Anorexia nervosa (often referred to as simply anorexia) is characterized by a significant weight loss due to a purposeful attempt to stop eating. The anorexic, intensely fearful of becoming obese, considers herself to be fat—no matter what her actual weight. Anorexics close to death at 65 pounds will show you where on their bodies they feel they need to lose weight. In an attempt to be even skinnier, the anorexic avoids taking in calories at all costs—even if the cost is her life.

Essential Features of Anorexia Nervosa

- Intense fear of becoming fat, which does not diminish as weight loss progresses
- Disturbance of body image (for example, claiming to "feel fat" even when emaciated)
- Significant weight loss (at least 15 percent of normal body weight)
- Refusal to maintain a minimal normal body weight
- No known physical illness that would account for the weight loss
- Amenorrhea (loss of menstruation) for at least three consecutive months (although in some cases, the menstrual pattern does not change; anorexia cannot be ruled out if someone is still menstruating)

Mariel's diary revealed the drastic nature of her dieting. When she was 16 years old and anorexic, she would write a daily entry in her diary listing the food she ate each day. This entry is typical:

10:00 a.m.	1 cup black coffee
	Sweet & Low
Noon	1 cup black coffee
	Sweet & Low
2:00 p.m.	1 vitamin A
	1 multiple vitamin
	1 vitamin B

7:00 p.m.	1 bouillon cube chicken broth and hot water
	1 Dietetic Jell-O (1 cup)

Mariel was 72 pounds and five feet, six inches. That she had already passed out twice by the time of this entry was no impediment to her harsh regimen.

The attempt to lose weight usually occurs through induced starvation, but anorexics can accelerate weight loss or undo the damage of occasional binges by vomiting, taking laxatives, using diuretics, or exercising rigorously. Severe dieting or exercising can lead to alteration in the body's fat-to-muscle ratio. This affects one's hormonal patterns, and changes in one's menstrual cycle usually result—sometimes even before a significant amount of weight has been lost. But amenorrhea does not always occur. Indeed, recently the criteria for anorexia have changed, no longer including amenorrhea as a prerequisite for the diagnosis.

Katie was a five foot, four inch 16-year-old who gained 25 pounds over six months following the breakup of a relationship with her boyfriend. In reaction to the loss of the relationship, she overate daily, avoiding friends and her usual social life. When she reached 145 pounds, however, she panicked at the weight gain and stopped eating. At home she would pick at her food, calculating the calories of each bite. What she actually put into her mouth was negligible. She insisted on eating only salads, and after meals she would figure out how many hours of exercise she needed to do that night to work off the fat. Sometimes she'd be up for hours before she felt she had burned off the calories. Within six weeks, Katie lost the weight she had gained as well as an additional 10 pounds. She was now 110 pounds, and she wanted to lose more weight. She had become terrified of putting anything in her mouth.

While Katie had not yet lost 15 percent of her normal body weight, her behavior was signaling a problem. The refusal to eat and consequent rapid weight loss, seeing herself as overweight despite her low weight, and her preoccupation with food and exercise were serious warning signs of anorexia nervosa. Her weight did not have to drop to 80 or 90 pounds for her to be considered eating disordered and in need of help.

How It Begins

No one starts a diet with the intention of becoming anorexic. The young woman who may ultimately find herself emaciated and near death starts out dieting like anyone else who wants to lose weight. However, for the person who is to become anorexic, the dieting and weight loss quickly take on a function that is unanticipated and unplanned. As this person begins to lose weight, she feels a newfound control in a life in which she previously did not feel effective or strong. Suddenly she feels powerful—she is able to make herself lose weight and look good. She does not have to give in to her hunger. She is someone who doesn't have to eat like other people do.

"When I'd be at dinner with my friends," says Margie, 17, of her months of anorexia, "I'd feel superior to everyone who was eating. I felt like I was the only one in control. The others were slaves to their hunger. It made me feel better than them."

The dieting and weight loss give meaning to the anorexic's life. Each day is a challenge—and every morning the number on the scale will say whether she has won or lost the previous day's contest. This challenge, this power, is not something that is a planned intention of the dieter but, once in effect, is hard for the anorexic to give up. The anorexic has often been the "good girl," accommodating to what others want of her. Now, perhaps for the first time, she has found a behavior that says, "You can't make me do what you want me to do. I'm not giving in to you—or to my hunger—or to my feelings. I'll eat what *I* want."

For the normally unassuming and shy anorexic, this is not an easy stance to abandon.

Who Is Vulnerable

The overwhelming majority 90 percent—of anorexics are women. The age at onset is usually between 12 and 18 years, but anorexia nervosa does occur in women in their forties and fifties, and we now, unfortunately, are seeing girls as young as 9 and 10 with anorexic behaviors. Approximately 0.5 to 1 percent of teenage and young adult women develop anorexia nervosa.[5]

There is as of yet no clear reason why one person becomes eating disordered and another does not. Current thinking indicates that eating disorders result from a complicated mix of biological, cultural, and psychological factors.

Susceptibility to anorexia nervosa, like susceptibility to all behaviors, is no doubt controlled in part by genetics. But at this time, little is understood about what aspects of inheritance account for anorexic behavior. One character trait often associated with anorexia is shyness. Obviously, not all shy girls become anorexic. But in some individuals becoming obsessed with their body size may be a way of attempting to overcome feelings of incompetence, unworthiness, and ineffectiveness, thus increasing their feelings of control over their lives.

We do now know that anorexia is associated with obsessive-compulsive disorder; therefore, the perfectionistic strivings common to anorexics may be a biologically determined component of this disorder. The preanorexic is the model child, rarely complaining, usually very helpful, compliant, and eager to please. Her school performance is often above average, and she is highly demanding and critical of herself. These qualities are obviously not always indications of a problem. For the anorexic, however, they are part of a bigger picture in which the perfection hides deep insecurities.

The anorexic is not someone with a comfortable sense of her own abilities, but rather someone who can never stop proving her competence. We don't know if this is psychologically derived or part of a more complex range of genetically determined compulsive drives. However, the perfectionism is usually carried over to one's personal relationships, where the anorexic often believes that in order to be cared about, she must always do the right thing—even if this means squelching her own feelings or acting in ways that make her feel uncomfortable. The anorexic is usually very private and keeps her feelings to herself, misleading others that all is well. But underneath the facade, there is deep trouble.

"I never felt like we really asked much of Zoe," her mother, Tina Camden, told us. "We didn't have to. She was always so bright and fun to be with—and very responsible. If Zoe had chores or responsibilities around the house, you knew they'd be done. You could count on it. She never complained like her brother or sisters. I never would have thought anything was wrong. Zoe's anorexia was a shock to everyone." At the time her mother spoke with us, Zoe, 15, was in an intensive care unit because of kidney failure secondary to the anorexia.

How the Disorder Progresses

While dieting may initially look normal, quickly it takes on a life of its own. There will be a preoccupation with food, dieting, and weight loss. Note that sometimes people who are not anorexic lose a lot of weight due to depression or a physical disorder, such as an intestinal problem. These problems may go undiagnosed and will result in the same type of extreme weight loss one sees in the anorexic. The difference is that in these cases the person is not actively attempting to be thinner. Whenever extreme weight loss occurs, a doctor should be contacted to rule out physical disorders or a psychological depression that might be the cause. Only in the case of an eating disorder will you see an active attempt at weight loss.

Someone who is anorexic will ask you if she looks fat. She will feel ashamed of being seen in public—because, at 90 pounds, she feels "disgustingly overweight." She may be on the scale 10 times a day.

Her diets will grow more and more extreme as time goes on. Often the anorexic will start with a normal diet, then eliminate one or two foods each day. If she can keep doing this, she feels pleased, sometimes elated that she has met her goals; if not, she is devastated, forlorn, hateful of herself "for being such a pig."

When Suzanne, 21, first came to treatment, she spoke of her experience this way:

> *Yesterday, for example, I had a grapefruit and black coffee for breakfast, and for dinner I had the normal salad I eat every night. I always skip lunch. I had promised myself that I would only eat three-quarters of the salad since I've been feeling stuffed after it lately—but I think I ate more than the three quarters. I know it was just lettuce and broccoli, but I can't believe I did that. I was up all night worrying about getting fat.*

Anorexics' conversations often center on food or looks. In fact, despite her own starvation, the anorexic often enjoys cooking, preparing meals for others, and collecting recipes. While she won't eat, her nutritional deprivation will result in constant thoughts about food. Many anorexics will even hide and hoard the food they won't eat.

Maria Jansen was looking through her daughter Jenny's bureau drawers for clothes to bring her after she had left to be hospitalized for anorexia. She was surprised to find one drawer packed with high-calorie sweets. It was a shock to her that Jennie could starve herself to near death and keep all that food at her fingertips.

Another particularly disturbing hallmark of anorexia nervosa is the persistent denial that anything is wrong. Hunger and fatigue are strongly denied. In fact, at a certain point, anorexics appear to genuinely lose the ability to feel hunger. When the disorder progresses to this stage, understandably it is extremely difficult for eating to be resumed without outside intervention. Physiological complications secondary to the anorexia are also ignored. Common medical problems can include dizziness, numbness of hands and feet, dehydration, and low blood pressure. Heart irregularities or heart or kidney failure can occur as a result of potassium depletion and severe nutritional imbalances. Loss of concentration is also common. Despite this, anorexics are typically fiercely resistant to the idea of therapy because all attempts to help or intervene are seen as a way to make them eat.

As a result of the ferocity of the anorexic's denial and her tenacious hold on the disorder, the progression of anorexia nervosa can be tragic. Some women die. Studies estimate the long-term fatality rate to be over 10 percent.[6]

For some people, anorexia nervosa can become a chronic problem, almost a way of life, with the sufferer never regaining a healthy weight and being tormented by the terror of becoming obese, driven by compulsions to exercise and eat ritualistically. For most people who become anorexic, however, the disorder is an acute illness lasting months to a few years that can be treated effectively through a combination of psychological and medical care.

Bulimia Nervosa

Bulimia nervosa, commonly referred to as bulimia, is usually character-ized by bingeing—that is, eating large amounts of food in a short time. The binge is followed by an attempt to get rid of the food and conse-quent calories, in what is called the "purge." In some cases, the person doesn't binge per se but feels compelled to get rid of anything she's eaten beyond what she has determined is okay.

"When I dieted, bread was absolutely out of the question," says Lucy, now 24 years old, of her adolescent bulimic years.

> *If I had one bite of bread, just one, I felt as though I blew it! I'd stop lis-tening to whoever was talking to me at the table. I'd start thinking, How can I get rid of this? I'd worry about how fat I'd look, how I couldn't fit into my clothes. My head would be flooded with thoughts of what to do now—should I binge, since I'd already blown it? I had to undo what I'd done. The night was blown. I was a mess.*

You cannot tell that someone is bulimic by her weight. Bulimics may be slightly underweight or overweight, but they are usually within a normal range. However, within this range, you might see 10- to 15-pound weight fluctuations.

When someone is not bingeing or purging, the way she eats may vary. Some bulimics eat normally; others diet rigorously at all times. Regardless of what is being eaten, most bulimic women never feel com-fortable around food. Food is the enemy, and they are engaged in a constant battle.

Essential Features of Bulimia

- Binge eating accompanied by an awareness that the eating pattern is abnormal
- Repeated attempts to lose weight through severely restrictive diets; self-induced vomiting; use of laxatives, cathartics, enemas, colonics, diuretics, or medications; or excessive exercise
- Binge eating and purging occurring on average at least twice weekly for three months
- Fear of not being able to stop eating voluntarily
- Depressed mood
- Self-deprecating thoughts following eating binges
- Self-evaluation that is overly influenced by body shape and weight

The Binge

A binge usually refers to the rapid consumption of a large amount of high-caloric food in a relatively short time. Binges can range anywhere from the intake of 1,000 to 60,000 calories or higher. However, sometimes a bulimic will consider a small amount of food, such as a piece of cake, to be a "binge." A binge can consist of just about anything you can imagine and may depend on what's available in terms of food and/or finances. Some people will binge occasionally, while for others, bingeing will take up a major portion of every day.

Some bulimics go to restaurants, order a full-course meal, throw up, then go to another restaurant and eat again. Three or four full-size meals may be eaten before the person feels exhausted enough to return home. And yes, it can be terribly costly. We have treated some women whose addiction to food was so extreme that the binges cost them upwards of

$100 to $150 a day. When the binges are this costly or when money is not readily available, as in the case of a child or a teenager, the bulimic may steal to support her food habit. In the most extreme cases, women have prostituted themselves to keep the food habit going.

Bingeing usually occurs in secret. It may be planned in advance, or it may be the case that any unplanned eating, even one bite, can lead to the feeling that the damage has been done. The bulimic is always trying to control her urges to eat. The consequent feelings of deprivation or the upset she feels when any control is relinquished often precipitates a binge.

Once a binge begins, bulimics will ravage their kitchen for food, go to the grocery store, or order in food from local restaurants. Or they will find food in other ways. One shy 18-year-old told us that when she vacationed with her parents, she'd steal food from the room service carts in the hallways of hotels. Another woman, a Wall Street executive who dressed impeccably and was very well mannered, described nightmarish evenings of rummaging for food through garbage bins in the back halls of her apartment building. She resorted to this behavior because she had ordered in food so often in the middle of the night that she could no longer stand her feelings of humiliation when met with her doorman's puzzled looks.

For some, bingeing occurs only at night when one wakes and eats—sometimes consciously, sometimes not. The missing food in the morning may be the only way the person knows that she had had a rough time with food the night before.

Whenever a binge takes place, all feelings are blocked out. The food acts as an anesthetic. As one bulimic woman put it:

I go to never-never land. Once I start bingeing, it's like being in a stupor, like being drunk. Nothing else matters. Heaven help the person who tries to stop me. It's like I'm a different person. It's very humiliating—but not then, not while I'm eating. While I'm eating, nothing else matters.

After the Binge: Shame and Panic

The binge leaves the bulimic exhausted and uncomfortable—not just physically, but emotionally as well. She is besieged with feelings of shame and guilt. She doesn't recognize the person she becomes during the binge and despises herself. She loathes this out-of-control, needy person. As one client expressed it, "I can't believe I can turn into a creature that acts in such an animal-like way."

Bulimics consider their bingeing disgusting and are deeply ashamed of it. It goes against the grain of who they are and what they are striving to be.

In addition to being ashamed, they are terrified about weight gain from whatever has been eaten, regardless of whether or not a large amount of food has been consumed. Bulimics are so perfectionistic in their standards of themselves that weight gain from the binge is never tolerated. They fear that any extra pounds will expose their other side, the person who binges and loses control. This is a frightening thought.

As Mary Anna, 28, told us:

I would die if people knew. Everyone thinks my life is so good. No one would believe I stuff down boxes of cake and cookies each night. If I gained weight, they'd see something was wrong—it would be a tip-off. I can't let anyone see how needy and desperate I get.

The awful feelings of shame, panic about weight gain, and physical discomfort lead the bulimic to the purge—the means of undoing the damage of the binge.

The Purge

Purging can take different forms. Most often it involves vomiting or laxative abuse. Other forms of purging are the use of diuretics, enemas, and colonics; fasting, strict dieting, and rigorous exercising; the misuse of diet pills; and amphetamine or cocaine abuse (these latter to suppress hunger on days following a binge).

The amount of purging varies from person to person. Some people binge and vomit a few times a month, others over 20 times a day. Sometimes the vomiting is induced in the middle of a binge so the eating can continue. Other times, the person vomits only after all the food has been consumed. Vomiting as a solution begins benignly, almost by accident, and only gradually does it become a ritualistic part of the bulimic cycle.

For Juliana, vomiting was a "solution" to her struggle to keep her weight down. She had been thin as a child, but during adolescence her body filled out, and she became self-conscious about her size. By the time she left for college, she was about 15 pounds overweight, and those 15 pounds were a major barrier to her self-confidence. Away from home and the seduction of her mother's kitchen, Juliana made a commitment to diet, and she stuck to it. She rigidly stayed on her food plan for three months and steadily approached her desired goal of 110 pounds.

By spring of her freshman year, Juliana thought of herself as a "new person." She had a new body, a new wardrobe—and a newfound terror of regaining weight. She couldn't stay on the diet forever.

> *I remember coming home from a party. I had eaten a lot there, and I felt fat and disgusting. I don't know why I thought of it then, but I remembered some friend of mine telling me how she threw up to lose weight. I*

decided to try it. I didn't really let myself think too much about what I was going to do or else it would have seemed too disgusting. But I used my fingers, and then it was done. I felt so relieved, so thin. I couldn't believe it was that easy. It was like magic.

For bulimics, the purge is the antidote to their loss of control over food. As one patient put it, "When I binge, I lose. When I purge, the food loses."

In all cases, the vomiting is induced; it doesn't "just happen." At first, vomiting is forced—by using fingers, a spoon handle, or Ipecac (an over-the-counter drug usually used by parents to induce vomiting in their children after accidental poisoning). After repeated vomiting, however, the esophageal muscles relax so much that many women don't have to do anything but tighten their stomachs, and they will be able to bring up the food.

The use of laxatives as a purging technique usually begins when someone takes one or two laxatives to get rid of the feeling that her stomach is full. Most laxative abusers have difficulty vomiting and turn to this method instead. The irony about laxative abuse is that by the time the laxatives work, the food has already been digested and the calories absorbed. Thus, laxative use gives the illusion of weight loss (since water weight is lost), but in actuality, calories are still retained, and weight is put on.

Yet even when laxative users know this, they often continue the abuse as a means of "feeling" thinner or flattening their stomach by purging themselves of water in the body. They refuse to believe it isn't working to control weight. Laxative use can quickly become laxative abuse. The body builds a tolerance, and one or two tablets a day will quickly lose their effectiveness. Often by the time a bulimic seeks help, she may be taking anywhere from 20 to 200 laxatives daily.

Enemas, diuretics, and colonics are used like laxatives to eliminate a feeling of fullness by facilitating or speeding up the body's usual functioning. Even though they may allow for an immediate sense of thinness and calm, in truth these purging techniques are ineffective in reducing calorie intake.

In some cases, the terror of gaining weight results in a compulsion to chew and spit out food. If one bite of food is actually swallowed, panic ensues. Huge quantities of food can be tasted this way, but nothing is actually ingested. Of course, depending on how much food is eaten at other times during the day, this torturous behavior can lead to anorexic weight loss despite the ongoing presence of food.

Other forms of purging—diet pills, drug use, fasting, and rigorous exercise—are used to inhibit eating or to burn off the calories after a binge.

John, 24, one of the male bulimics seen through our center, had a pattern of bingeing continuously for a week or two following a disappointment or frustration in his life. During this time, he ate throughout the day, would miss work, stopped shaving and caring for himself, and could easily put on 20 pounds. At a certain point of exhaustion or self-disgust (it was never clear to him when this would occur), he would stop bingeing and begin to eat healthfully, but he would also begin exercising in what was almost a panic-stricken manner. One hour of swimming preceded 10 miles of fast-paced jogging. A strenuous workout ritual was what he had to look forward to when he returned home from work. If John was lax in any of these regimens, he became severely self-critical and anxious and was plagued with thoughts of gaining weight. John's exercise regimen was as drastic a purge as vomiting was for the women previously mentioned.

How It Begins—"It Won't Happen to Me"

No one who decides to control weight by vomiting, laxative use, or any other forms of purging ever believes that she will end up in an out-of-control cycle of bingeing and purging. In fact, bulimia always starts out as a way of being *in* control—in control of food, of weight, of one's size, of one's image.

"I didn't think it was really such a bad thing," said Rachel, 38 and bulimic for 20 years. "When I first started purging, I'd throw up about once or twice a month, when I decided I didn't want to keep down what I'd eaten. I figured other people smoked, or drank, or did drugs. I didn't do any of those things, so I figured they all had their thing; this was mine."

But what happened to Rachel was fairly typical. Knowing she could vomit provided the excuse to give in to the urge to eat more and more often, until she was caught up in a desperate cycle of bingeing and purging that reached its current twice-daily frequency.

No matter the method, purging provides the perfect solution for the bulimic. It allows her to continue to eat not merely to satisfy physical hunger, but more importantly to meet emotional needs. An addictive cycle develops in which she relies on the binge and purge as a part of her daily life. The cycle cannot be stopped easily. Once it begins, despite starting out as the perfect solution, the eating and purging become terrifying and dreaded, like (as one patient put it) a sadistic lover you can't leave.

Who Is Vulnerable

Bulimia usually starts in adolescence or young adulthood, although recently the age at onset is occurring in girls as young as 11 or 12 and in women in their forties and fifties. The binge–purge cycle often begins at transition points of independence, such as beginning to date, leaving for college, or getting married, when stress is high and there are no clear outlets for emotional conflict and tension. Another common precipitant to the binge–purge cycle is the breakup of a relationship with a boyfriend or spouse.

As with the other eating disorders, bulimia develops as a result of complex biopsychosocial factors. Research indicates that physiological components may play a role in cravings and the need to purge. Additionally, the culture helps foster problematic beliefs regarding weight and body image. Like anorexics, bulimics tend to be people who do not feel secure about their own self-worth. They feel dependent on others for approval and appreciation and rely on others' judgments to determine their worthiness. Because they are so vulnerable to what others think of them, these women are more susceptible to the culture's messages of how they should look.

Bulimic women tend to be conforming and eager to please, hiding anger, upset, or other negative feelings from themselves and others, except perhaps in the safety of one's own home. There, someone may indeed be angry, even at times tyrannical! But it may remain unclear what is really of concern. Running to one's room and slamming the door because homework has to be done, for example, may cover the more raw feelings of not having been chosen for the soccer team. Turning to food may then become an outlet for all the feelings and conflicts that cannot be tolerated, exposed, or perhaps even known.

Approximately 1 to 3 percent of adolescent and young adult females in the United States develop bulimia.[7] At least 90 percent of bulimics are women. However, it is possible that there are more men who are bulimic, but, because they are less likely to seek treatment, there are no reliable statistics on them. One reason for this is the shame men who binge and vomit experience for having a "women's disease." Others who exercise to offset binges may deny they have a problem. Men who engage in vigorous sports, such as marathon running, to control their weight may be eating disordered. When exercise has become a way to compensate for weight gain from bingeing, and a cycle of overeating and exercising becomes a way of dealing with stress, an eating disorder has developed. Excessive body building, especially with the use of steroids, can be a sign of psychological trouble. Here, a focus on the body may not be an attempt at improving fitness. Instead, enlarging one's size may be a means of compensating for poor self-esteem or other emotional concerns. However, given that exercising is not usually in and of itself worrisome (whereas vomiting is), women, not men, fill the treatment rooms.

How the Disorder Progresses

What starts out as an attempt to control one's body and weight quickly becomes behavior that is out of control. Initially, turning to food actually works to make the bulimic feel calmer and less under pressure when she is upset. Because it works, the bulimia becomes entrenched as a way of coping with uncomfortable emotional states.

Someone who is bulimic thinks more and more about eating and purging. She begins to structure her day around when she'll eat, what she'll eat, and how she can get rid of the calories. The bulimia inevitably takes on a life of its own, and the person no longer feels that she is choosing to binge or vomit but that the binge–purge cycle has gained control.

Louisa, 18, talked tearfully of trying to get through the days at college struggling with bulimia:

Every day I wake up and say I'm going to be "good" today. Usually I make it until dinner without bingeing or getting sick, but the evenings are always the worst. Sometimes I actually make it to bed—but then I lie there not being able to sleep. I keep thinking if I just ate a little it would put me to sleep. Sometimes I'll toss and turn till three or four a.m., but I always end up giving in and eating my roommate's food or even going out to the candy machines at school. Even if I only eat one thing, like a muffin or one candy bar, I have to throw it up, or it will sit in my stomach and I can't sleep. What kills me is that every day for three years I've been doing this—starting out "good" and then blowing it every night. Do you know how that makes me feel? I feel like something crazy is happening to me. Am I going to spend the rest of my life fighting with this thing?

Another woman, Annie, in her thirties, told us of a tormented struggle to stop the bingeing and get the bulimia out of her life:

I feel like a prisoner in my own life. I can't have one thing in the refrigerator, or I know when I come home from work I'll eat it. One night all I had in the refrigerator was one onion. The refrigerator was completely bare except for this stupid onion. I had already eaten dinner and had vowed not to eat anything more, but this onion kept haunting me. Finally at midnight I gave in and sautéed it with some oil I had. That was it—I had blown it. After that I ordered in $30 worth of Chinese food. That rotten onion was the start of a three-hour binge.

Other women describe putting Ajax on food that they don't want to eat, dumping food in the garbage, and having parents or roommates hide or lock up food. This is always to no avail. Food is washed, dug up from under the trash, or found no matter where the hiding place is. The struggle not to binge is as profound as the struggle for any addict trying to kick a habit.

It is a common experience for a bulimic to start the day with the vow "Not today. Today I won't binge." Such vows are well meaning but ignore the complexities of the bulimic's relationship to food and how great the emotional need is for it. As soon as the promise is made, all she can think about is food, and the temptation to binge is heightened.

The bulimic caught in the struggle with food often doesn't realize that she has a treatable disorder. She thinks it is a personal failing and lives with the torture of self-contempt. Unlike the anorexic, the bulimic *does* acknowledge she's hurting herself. She admits to her psychological distress and often knows of the physiological consequences of her behavior. Medical complications can include fatigue, sore throat, ulcerated esophagus, tooth decay, and, worse, heart disturbances due to potassium depletion. Laxative abuse, in particular, can lead to constipation, gastrointestinal bleeding, rectal prolapse, and a physiological dependence on the laxatives in order to evacuate. But even when the bulimic is aware of these complications, she does not use them as motivators to change. Instead, these problems are seen as proof that she is a terrible person. "Look at what I'm doing to myself," we frequently hear. "I'm slowly killing myself, and I won't even stop."

Complications that lead to death are less common in bulimia, but if treatment is not pursued, bulimia can become a lifelong progressive disorder in which more and more of the person's daily activities and thoughts are oriented around food. However, because the bulimic does know something is wrong, over time she is more likely than her anorexic "sister" to seek help to change her behavior.

Binge-Eating Disorder

Binge-eating disorder is characterized by uncontrollable eating followed by feelings of guilt and shame.

Binge eating without purging inevitably results in weight gain. Yet, not everyone who is overweight has an eating disorder. We are frequently asked by parents who notice their child's weight gain whether their son or daughter has an eating disorder. The answer is not necessarily.

Indeed, binge-eating disorder is often confused with obesity. *Obesity* is a term used when someone weighs more than 25 percent above her expected normal body weight or when the person's body mass index (BMI) is greater than 30. According to some estimates, half of all Americans are overweight, and a quarter are obese. Weight gain can result from a poor diet, lack of exercise, or genetic factors. Research indicates, however, that only 1 to 4 percent of the public reports symptoms of binge-eating disorder.[8]

Binge eating is a psychological disorder in which someone is using food to cope with stress, emotional distress, and daily problems. The eating may start out as pleasurable, but it quickly feels out of control and is experienced as abnormal. Someone who likes snacks, lives on carbohydrates and soft drinks, and can't resist desserts is not necessarily a binge eater. However, if food is hoarded in one's room or car, if someone urgently stuffs herself when no one is looking, if food is no longer enjoyed but obsessively craved—then a problem may indeed exist. Like bulimics, binge eaters do recognize that there is something wrong.

When someone is bingeing, dieting is mistakenly seen as the solution and is undertaken with strenuous effort. Feelings of deprivation set in because the dieting is usually approached in a rigid manner. The feelings of deprivation soon give way to a veering from the diet, and the consequent despair over "blowing it" results in a return to the binge eating. The problem often becomes cyclical and never ending because the dieting misses the point. Unless the psychological reasons for the compulsive behavior are also addressed, there is much less chance that healthy eating will be sustained.

Essential Features of Binge-Eating Disorder

- Binge eating accompanied by an awareness that the eating pattern is abnormal
- Fear of not being able to stop eating voluntarily
- Bingeing that occurs, on average, two days weekly for at least six months
- Depressed mood
- Self-deprecating thoughts following the binges

How It Starts

Unlike anorexia and bulimia, binge eating generally has a more gradual beginning. It often starts in early childhood when eating patterns are formed. Sometimes food is used early on as a retreat from feelings, as a way to feel good, or as an activity to fill otherwise empty time. Eating patterns that do not create weight gain for the growing child can result in weight problems when the person stops growing. When binge eating starts in young adulthood, it is often at times of stress when the person feels ill equipped to handle certain frustrations and emotions.

Who Is Vulnerable

Binge eating, like bulimia and anorexia nervosa, is a complicated disorder with psychological, physiological, and cultural factors contributing to its development.

We are in a culture in which we are constantly surrounded by the availability of rich, super-sized portions of food. Yet, the culture also insists on deprivation—in the face of all that food, women (and men now too) are supposed to achieve model-like bodies. Attempts to meet the values of the culture can result in depriving diets. The impossibility of meeting one's goals can ultimately result in giving up and bingeing.

Everyone knows at times what it means to eat "too much." However, for some, the craving to eat more can feel overpowering. We now know that cravings can be physiologically derived, with serotonin depletion accounting for some of these urges. In these cases, the cravings may be more extreme than they are for others. Here, food acts as a drug to help calm what otherwise feels to be an out-of-control sense of urgent need.

As with anorexia nervosa and bulimia, binge eating becomes problematic for those who do not have other ways of dealing with cravings, upset, stress, or the complicated messages our society generates.

Unlike the other two disorders, there is a high proportion of male binge eaters. Treatment, however, is sought one and a half times more frequently by women than men.[9] It is also a common clinical observation that binge eating runs in families. People who are vulnerable often come from families in which there is an overemphasis on food and how much someone eats.

"In my family, how much you appreciated a dinner was measured by how much you ate. Whether you actually felt hungry never mattered," said one binge eater. Another woman told us, "Whether I cared about starving children or hurting my mother's feelings was the incentive to eat. No one seemed to pay attention to appetite."

How the Disorder Progresses

Binge-eating disorder is often a chronic syndrome that remains with someone for life. It can start very subtly, with a child turning to food whenever she is upset. Over time, that person learns that food in fact will soothe her. It works to block out feelings or to calm her down—but at a terribly high price. The psychological torment involved in this disorder can also be combined with physiological complications from poor dietary habits and consequent weight gain. Physical problems can include such difficulties as heart ailments, mobility problems, and diabetes. Yet, as with any drug, bingeing is turned to despite its toll. The destructive pattern continues because the person has not established other ways of dealing with cravings, or she has not learned to trust that feelings pass and that she is capable of soothing herself without the food.

Like a bulimic, the binge eater has usually tried to stop in every way possible. Often the attempt at control is rigorous dieting and living by a system of absolutes. This inflexible system leaves no room for deviation. When the binge eater goes off a self-imposed diet, the rigidity collapses, and she feels all is lost. The feelings of guilt, shame, and failure that follow are the same that plague bulimics.

Diets and weight loss procedures may help intermittently, but in the long run, if they don't touch the emotional reasons for bingeing, they may not work. In fact, for some binge eaters, stringent dieting is the first step toward the binge. The experience of deprivation is the precursor to wanting food. There is no better way to create a craving than through deprivation. A pattern of bingeing and dieting can go on indefinitely when dieting is erroneously seen as the only solution to the problem.

Binge eating has only recently been taken seriously in our culture. However, prejudicial impressions remain strong. Binge eaters are considered lazy and gluttonous or, at best, lacking in willpower or self-control. Binge eating is as serious a problem as bulimia or anorexia in terms of the toll it takes on someone's life, and it should be treated as such.

Sharon, a 24-year-old binge eater, shared her distraught feelings with us:

> *I keep going to different eating disorder groups and facilities, and it's clear I don't belong there. I don't throw up, I'm not too thin, I'm not a perfectionist about my size and looks. Then when I try going to a diet group like Weight Watchers, it's clear I don't belong there either. It's not simply a matter of dieting for me. I know how to diet. I don't know how to stop the binges. It seems wherever I go, I have the wrong problem. I can't even get this right.*

Without the obviously strange and damaging behavior of vomiting, the binge eater and those around her are less likely to identify her problem as serious. It often seems to her and others that the problem is one of too big an appetite or a stubborn lack of self-control. This mislabeling of the problem can keep the cycle going for years. Only when psychological factors are considered along with a healthy diet can behavior change be sustained.

What You Can Observe—and What You Can't

This chapter has focused on illuminating the observable aspects of eating disorders. Many people do not fit neatly into one category or the other. Some people exhibit traits from more than one category. Other people may change their behavior over time; for example, they start out with symptoms that typify the anorexic and move into behaviors that are more characteristic of the bulimic.

In many situations serious eating problems go on far too long without notice. The following checklists will help you identify a situation that deserves your attention. The importance of educating yourself and having a clearer picture of what you are observing is not to categorize, but to have the information you will need to deal effectively with the situation.

The checklists describe signs of the three eating disorders that may be visible to the outside observer. These lists are not all-inclusive of every symptom but instead focus on what you can observe. Check the signs that you've seen under each category. It is not important whether or not you are able to diagnose which eating disorder your friend or loved one is suffering from; just note what it is that you see. In some cases, the problem will be strikingly clear. In others, this information can be used to help a professional make a diagnostic determination. We will refer back to the information from these checklists in later chapters. Remember, though, that some of the most critical characteristics of an eating disorder are those you won't be able to see—the unspoken sadness, confusion, and fears. Those more complicated signs will be addressed in the chapters to follow.

Checklist for Visible Characteristics of Anorexia Nervosa

Behavioral Signs

___Signs of restricted eating (unusually low intake of food), such as severe diets or fasting

___Odd food rituals, such as counting bites of food, cutting food into tiny pieces, or preparing food for others while refusing to eat

___Intense fear of becoming fat, regardless of low weight

___Fear of food and situations where food may be present

___Rigid exercise regimens

___Dressing in layers to hide weight loss

___Bingeing

___Use of laxatives, enemas, or diuretics to get rid of food

___Frequent weighing

Physiological Signs

___Weight loss (often in a short period of time)

___Cessation of menstruation without physiological cause

___Paleness

___Complaints of feeling cold or tired

___Dizziness and fainting spells

Attitude Shifts

___Mood shifts

___Perfectionistic attitude

___Insecurities about capabilities regardless of actual performance

___Feelings of self-worth determined by what is or is not eaten

___Withdrawal from people

Checklist for Visible Characteristics of Bulimia Nervosa

Behavioral Signs

____Bingeing

____Secretive eating, evidenced by missing food

____Preoccupation with and constant talk about food and/or weight

____The avoidance of restaurants, planned meals, or social events if food is present

____Self-disparagement when too much has been eaten

____Bathroom visits after meals

____Vomiting, laxative abuse, or fasting

____The use of diet pills

____Rigid and harsh exercise regimens

____Fear of being fat, regardless of weight

Physiological Signs

____Swollen glands, puffiness in the cheeks, or broken blood vessels under the eyes

____Complaints of sore throat

____Complaints of fatigue and muscle ache

____Unexplained tooth decay

____Frequent weight fluctuations, often within a 10- to 15-pound range

Attitude Shifts

____Mood shifts that include depression, sadness, guilt, and self-hate

____Severe self-criticism

____The need for approval (including yours) to feel good about herself

____Self-worth determined by weight

Checklist for Characteristics of Binge-Eating Disorder

Behavioral Signs

____Bingeing or frequent grabbing of food

____Restriction of activities because of embarrassment about weight

____Going from one diet to the next

____Eating little in public while maintaining a high weight

Physiological Signs

____Weight gain

____Weight-related hypertension or fatigue

Attitude Shifts

____Feelings about self based on weight and control of eating

____Fantasizing about being a better person when thin

____Feeling tormented by eating habits

____Social and professional failures attributed to weight

____Weight is the focus of life.

2

Hidden Feelings

The Psychological Aspects of
Eating Disorders

When Joyce, a 23-year-old bulimic, came to our center for a treatment consultation, she explained her situation this way: "I have a nice apartment, a good job, a terrific boyfriend. Everything would be going okay if it weren't for the bingeing and vomiting. I've tried to make myself stop, but I can't. If you could just help me get rid of the bulimia, I'd be okay. I'm worried it's going to ruin my health."

Joyce was upset and confused by her eating disorder. Why was she bingeing even though it was so offensive to her? Was she lacking in willpower or strength of character? When they learned of Joyce's eating disorder, her parents were also confused. Joyce seemed to have everything going for her. What was wrong? Joyce herself didn't know. All she knew was that she couldn't stop bingeing and didn't want to be fat. She would relieve the awful fullness by vomiting. For Joyce, the reasons she was compelled to binge and vomit were as unknown to her as they were to those observing her.

What's Going On Inside?

An eating disorder is not merely a problem with food or weight. It is an attempt to use food intake and weight control to solve unseen emotional conflicts or difficulties that in fact have little to do with either food or weight. An eating disorder is *never* simply a matter of self-control. Healthier eating habits and stronger willpower are not the missing ingredients that will make the problem disappear.

Anorexia nervosa, bulimia nervosa, and binge eating never exist in a vacuum. These disorders do not occur in an otherwise satisfied, productive, and emotionally healthy person. At first this may be a very hard concept to accept. Often people hope for something like a surgical procedure that will "cut out" the behavior the way a surgeon removes diseased tissues or organs. However, it is a destructive myth that the only problem is the eating behavior.

After years of failed efforts to stop bingeing and vomiting, Joyce joined a support group to help her resist her strong urges to binge. After several months in this group and when she was feeling less isolated and frightened, Joyce was able to pay attention to the connection between her eating and her feelings of anger and discomfort:

> *I always thought the bingeing just came over me. But then one day I was lying in bed really angry at my mother for a conversation we had just had. I was so angry I could barely deal with it. Then all of a sudden I noticed that I was thinking about what I wanted to eat. It was amazing. I realized I had calmed down, wasn't angry anymore—all I wanted to do was binge.*

Jill, a 17-year-old anorexic, describes her experience:

When I was starving myself, all I felt was that I had to. There was no rhyme or reason to it. You could not have convinced me it had anything to do with something emotional or psychological. It took time for me to see how frightened I was and how I had to feel in absolute control. It seems strange now, even a little pathetic, but my eating was all I could control: I felt I was more powerful than anyone when I wasn't eating. What a peculiar way to feel competent.

Is She Trying to Hurt Herself?

"But it's so destructive. Is she trying to hurt herself?" Joyce's mother wanted to know. The question is a common one. Eating disorders are destructive. They take a great toll, emotionally and physically. But this is not by design. Only when you understand the ways in which an eating disorder is someone's attempt to deal with feelings or to feel better about herself can you see that the destructiveness is a by-product of the problem, not an intent. In fact, the self-destructiveness of binge eating and bulimia causes the individual great anguish and is often a motivator to stop.

"Tell me *again* about the side effects and risks of death," requested a bulimic patient. "Maybe if I can really focus on how I am hurting myself, I can finally stop."

With another patient, it took years of intensive therapy for her to see and accept that her weight was part of a solution to an emotional problem. "I always thought the weight was the obstacle. It was what kept me from a happy life. Indeed, at 280 pounds, I and everyone else thought I was just out to kill myself—a slow suicide. It is only recently that I've begun to see that my deeper terror is that of feeling close to people—I built a natural barrier. No wonder every time I lost weight I ran right back to food."

In anorexia, the destructiveness is flatly denied. Even on the brink of death, the anorexic sees her starving as essential to her sense of competence and self-esteem. It feels necessary to life, even as it kills.

In every eating disorder, it is only when the person is able to find healthier means of taking care of herself and generating internal sources of self-esteem that she can give up the attempts at coping that have, ironically and tragically, led to further emotional and physical damage. Only by understanding the protective and adaptive functions of these behaviors can *you* begin to appreciate why it may be so hard for someone to just "give it up."

An Eating Disorder Is an External Solution to Inner Turmoil

A focus on body size is a way to convert a worry about something inside to something outside. For example, if the concern "Am I good enough?" becomes "Am I thin enough?" the sufferer creates an external and measurable scale of her self-worth that offers her a less painful and more comprehensible way to cope with her fears.

In a now quite famous study, researcher Catherine Steiner-Adair evaluated preteens to consider which young girls were most vulnerable to developing disordered eating. The girls were first asked what they thought women were supposed to be in our culture. "We're supposed to get married, have kids, have a profession, be beautiful . . ." they answered. Then they were asked what goals they had for themselves.

The girls divided into two general groups. Some girls, despite the likely impossibility of the goals, said that they essentially wanted it all: to be beautiful, to be a mother, to be successful—essentially to be a superwoman.. Others seemed more discerning: they would get a career, have kids later. Or maybe they would focus on having a family—what they really wanted more than anything was to be a mom. The girls were then given eating disorder questionnaires. Interestingly, the girls who wanted to be superwomen showed significant signs of becoming eating disordered. The girls who had more of a sense of themselves, who had thought about what they wanted, not what the culture wanted, clearly were less troubled about their bodies and food.[10]

The implication of this study is that for girls who become eating disordered, there is a lack of confidence regarding their own feelings, values, and self-worth. They turn to the outside world—be it the culture's values, their boyfriends' wishes, the scale, their parents—to determine how—and whom—they should be.

In general, young girls, more so than their male counterparts, are often encouraged to pay attention to others' needs before listening to their own. As a result, they may keep a good deal of their feelings, wishes, and needs private and secret—sometimes even secret from themselves. Angry, aggressive feelings are seen as bad and unacceptable rather than the basis of healthy assertion. Because of this, many young girls feel as though they're "bad" for having these feelings.

Girls who become eating disordered have taken these messages to an extreme. The good girl is the quiet, unseen girl who learns not to show what is bothering her. She hides her emotions, even as her disorder progresses. She learns to feel good about herself through pleasing others, while her own "appetites" are suppressed. What other people want seems justified; what she wants is a sign of selfishness.

Betty, a 30-year-old bulimic, began to discover that the eating disorder was more about feeling secure than about food:

> It started to dawn on me that the bingeing and purging weren't entirely about my weight—and then I noticed a certain pattern. When I was with a man, I was not bingeing. If someone was sleeping in my bed at night, there was no urge to binge. It wasn't just that I couldn't binge because someone was there, but that the urge was gone. I noticed this when I started keeping a journal of my feelings and experiences, and it floored me. If a man likes me, I feel pretty and confident. If no one is there, I feel awful about myself—as if I am two different people. It's bizarre to me that a stranger can completely change the way I feel about myself.

Anxiety

People with eating disorders have difficulty using anxiety as a signal to cope. As strange as it may seem, anxiety can be a very useful tool, alerting us to situations or events that make us feel vulnerable. And with this awareness we can marshal our coping skills.

For example, if the idea of an upcoming exam makes us anxious, the tension and uneasiness can be a powerful motivator to study. Anxiety provides the opportunity to prepare for the event by anticipating the possible roadblocks and giving us the opportunity to *act* to protect ourselves in potentially difficult situations.

But people with eating disorders often feel that anxiety is a signal of impending doom, a flag that whatever is coming will be emotionally overwhelming. They feel that anxiety is something to be gotten rid of, not listened to. Here is where families and significant others often run into trouble. Sensing the tension that ensues when a loved one is anxious, family members can rush in to make the anxiety and stress go away. A cycle of dependency is encouraged if not completely cemented into the relationships. While everyone needs support at times, this kind of relationship can result in someone never having the confidence to listen to herself and know her own needs. When there is upset or trouble, the person scrambles to have someone else calm her down. When another person isn't around, food can become the next likely substitute. Therefore, the experience of anxiety is often the trigger to binge or, as in the case of anorexia, to starve. While these behaviors numb the anxiety, they do nothing to help the person prepare for or protect against the actual cause of the anxiety.

An Eating Disorder Is a Form of Substance Abuse

In Betty's case, she was able to substitute a man for the food in order to define how she felt about herself and calm herself down. A man was a scale of sorts, telling her if she was good enough. He was also a warm, soothing body rather than a complex human being to interact with. In this way, a man was like a substance rather than a person. Be it a man or a binge, Betty was relying on an external substance to alleviate her inner distress. When used for emotional purposes, food functions like a drug or alcohol: It provides escape.

As time goes on, food can replace people, and the isolation increases. Said one 19-year-old college student who would binge and vomit several times nightly:

> It got to be so that I would rather spend a Saturday night eating than with
> my friends. Being with people felt superficial. I was just killing time till I

could go home and eat. I'd be carrying on a perfectly normal conversa-
tion, but in the back of my mind, all I'd be thinking about was all the food
I could eat as soon as I left. I knew something was wrong. I hated that
food was so important, but I was trapped. I couldn't get the thoughts of
food out of my head, and I didn't know any way out.

Loneliness

When someone is constantly turning to outside sources to find out who she is and how she should act, being alone can be empty and terrifying. Eating (or sometimes starving) can temporarily soothe this kind of painful experience.

Jim, a binge eater, felt condemned to loneliness. His self-consciousness about his weight kept him from taking part in activities and events. He thought everyone would be as disgusted at the sight of him as he was when he looked at himself.

"When I'm at home alone," said Jim, "I get so lonely, it becomes a physical emptiness inside. Planning what to eat becomes an activity—it's like planning whom I'll spend time with."

For some, loneliness is felt as boredom. This feeling can occur despite the presence of other people. "I feel so lost," Maddie, 21 years old and bulimic, said of her evenings:

I'll be fine during the day, as long as I'm busy, but as soon as I'm home at
night, nothing seems to satisfy me. I feel empty, lost, this sense of vague
uneasiness. I try to read or work, but I feel distracted, ungrounded. I want
to be "filled up." I know my family is there, and I can spend time with
them, but that doesn't do it for me. Sometimes drugs or alcohol seems to
take away that feeling. Other times, if I sleep with a guy, that might do

it too. But whether it's food, drugs, guys, or booze, it's always temporary, leaving me feeling horrible about myself afterward. And empty still.

These feelings are often intensified when people are in fact alone. Some people experience being alone as though they were abandoned, left behind. Thoughts of food or exercise regimens—or, for the anorexic, the fierce battle not to eat—can be an oddly satisfying kind of company at such empty times.

She May Also Be Depressed

Many people with eating disorders grapple with low moods, low energy levels, and feelings of despondency and sadness.

In some cases, the intensity of the mood and the seriousness of associated behaviors, such as severe sleep problems, lack of interest in life, and constant self-deprecating thoughts, indicate the presence of a clinical depression.

Depression is usually associated with feelings of helplessness, ineffectiveness, loss of control, and/or unexpressed anger. The relationship between feeling depressed and eating disorders is a complicated one. Because bulimics and binge eaters often feel out of control, feeling depressed can be a frequent by-product of an eating disorder. After all, how would you feel if you repeatedly promised yourself to stop some destructive, disruptive behavior and failed over and over again?

For many people, depression and mood swings are the result of the disordered eating itself. Erratic and restrictive food intake can lead to internal chemical imbalances that can wreak havoc with mood. When this is the case, the mood swings and depressed feelings will be alleviated by a normal diet. But for some proportion of sufferers, the syndrome or illness of depression has preceded the eating disorder and may be physiologically based. In these cases, the eating disorder may be the attempt to alleviate or anesthetize against the depression to make it bearable. In fact, bingeing can actually raise the level of serotonin in the brain. Serotonin is a neurotransmitter that can result in the feeling of well-being and calm. Thus, for some, bingeing may be an attempt at self-medication, a means of providing temporary relief from dysphoric moods.[11]

Sara spoke of her periods of extreme depression:

These waves of lethargy and dullness would come over me. The day before I'd be fine, but then I would wake up and feel such utter hopelessness and despair that there would be no point in going to work or seeing friends. What seemed to offer pleasure yesterday looked bleak and uninviting today. I couldn't move, and I'd feel horrible about myself. I don't know what makes me feel like this. But once I start to feel this way, it goes on for weeks, and there is nothing I want to do but eat. And then it lifts—as mysteriously as it began—leaving me 10 to 20 pounds heavier.

Sara's bouts of depression began years before the bingeing became a part of her life. She had a history of depressive episodes, but as a child her depression manifested itself through sleep disturbances and crying spells. When Sara reached 11 or 12, she found that eating alone in her room seemed to comfort and calm her. Although she didn't know it, Sara's use of food was an attempt at medicating herself for a depression that no one knew existed. What started out as a naive attempt to deal with her depressive state quickly developed into bulimia.

Among the people for whom depression is associated with disordered eating, antidepressants can be a critical aspect of treatment. In Chapter 6, we discuss the use of medication and its treatment implications.

Fear of Others

Ironically, as lonely or depressed as they are, eating-disordered people are often more comfortable with food than they are with developing meaningful relationships. They can have great difficulty trusting people and relationships.

Some people fear losing themselves, their own identities, in their attempts to please another person. Others fear that the other person will take over, dominating them and leaving them little room to be themselves. This dilemma can make being in a relationship with someone who is eating disordered endlessly exasperating.

Jody, a 26-year-old binge eater, had trouble letting others get near her for fear she would give up control just as she always had with her mother:

> She was always doing things for me. It could be anything from changing batteries in my radio to cleaning up my room. I guess she was just taking care of me, but I felt like she was controlling everything, and I came to believe I couldn't take care of myself. Now I worry about this whenever I get close to anyone else. I like being taken care of, but I quickly feel controlled. I'm so confused about this that the second I even make plans with someone, I start to feel trapped.

Many recovered binge eaters have to contend with the fear of getting close to people after they have lost weight. Sexual intimacy is one aspect of emotional relatedness that can be avoided through bingeing and weight gain.

Said Cindy, a 34-year-old binge eater:

> I was so afraid to let a man near me. At 200 pounds, it wasn't much of

a worry. I wasn't even aware of my terror till I lost the weight and men began to notice me. Then what I had been avoiding all these years hit me. What an eye-opener—even at 120 pounds I felt inadequate and unworthy. So it wasn't the weight after all, it was me.

Anger and Aggression

Not surprisingly, if someone is in conflict about needing others—and needing to push them away—they often walk around the world angry and confused. Couple this with a fear that expressing feelings is at best problematic, and you have the picture of many eating-disordered young women.

Suzanne, 15, put it this way:

I got the message loud and clear that my brothers are allowed to disagree, fight, and be aggressive. Me? I'm supposed to be polite and make sure I don't hurt anyone's feelings. I guess I learned that in spades. As soon as I feel myself to be demanding or angry, I feel terrible and selfish. With food, though, I can let this out. I tear at it and eat with my hands. If anyone ever saw me, they wouldn't believe I'm the same person. I'm in my own world, and I don't care about anyone else. If they saw me, they'd know how selfish I can be, how angry, how I don't really care about anyone; it would be a disaster. But at least when I'm bingeing no one gets hurt—except, I guess, me.

A child or teenager in conflict about her natural feelings of anger and aggression grows up to be an adult with equal difficulties, only the context of her conflict broadens.

Jennifer, a 30-year-old corporate executive, describes how the requirements of her work clash head-on with her discomfort in asserting herself:

It's bizarre—here I am in charge of a whole department, and I'm uncom-
fortable with the idea of offending anyone, making anyone mad at me.
Whenever I have to assert myself, which is often at this job, I feel like I've .
done something wrong. Then I go straight for the food. Somehow when
I'm eating, I can forget about how badly it all makes me feel.

For the eating-disordered person who worries what others think of
her, the experience of anger and consequent aggression can be very
disruptive. Some people manage that experience by dissociating the
anger from themselves. This means that they feel like they become
someone else when they get angry or when they let out that anger
through bingeing.

Said Lettie, a 19-year-old bulimic:

It's like there is this horrible monster inside who takes over, and I can't
control it. When I'm in a bingeing phase, I'm like a different person. I'll
be nasty and not care about others. Usually I'm a very nice person—too
nice. Usually I'm the one who takes care of everyone else first, and my
own needs and feelings come last.

Other people have described this aspect of themselves as being "an
ogre," a "derelict," or "it's the dark side of me." One patient suggested
she was more in need of an exorcist than a therapist.

It is the "monster" who binges and thereby expresses parts of the
person that feel bad, out of control, ugly, and distasteful. In bulimia,
this monster is undone by purging; in anorexia, it is defeated by control. In either case, the feeling of being in a battle with oneself is a part
of daily life.

Someone with an eating disorder usually has a great deal of trouble
acknowledging, accepting, and enduring negative feelings like anger.
But sometimes it is the more tender emotions, like affection, longing,

and dependence, that cause problems. Sometimes one feeling conflicts with another, such as wanting to be grown up and wanting to remain a child at the same time. Feelings can be, and often are, intense for the eating-disordered person, who fears being overwhelmed by them or, worse still, overwhelming others with them. The fear of her feelings then exacerbates the problem, leading the person to panic and rush to food.

Need for Approval and Nurturance

People with eating disorders tend to be more dependent than others. This is true even when it doesn't look that way. The eating-disordered woman relies more than most of us on other people's opinions and reflections of her to determine how she feels about herself. This is why eating-disordered people are terrified of criticism. Criticism not only means that something they do or say is not approved of by others, but it can be taken as a judgment about whether they are a good or bad person.

As Lilly, a 25-year-old recovering anorexic, told us, "If someone didn't like a dress I wore, it didn't just mean that they didn't like the dress—it meant they didn't like *me*." She had not yet learned how to give herself the support and validation she needed, and thus she felt dependent on others to give her the approval that she couldn't give herself.

Not only is the eating-disordered person in need of approval, but inside she is "hungry" for care and affection as well. Often, she has been so attuned to everyone else's needs that her own have gotten overlooked.

Despite feelings of dependency, women with eating disorders don't want to rely on or need other people. Feeling dependent or needy leaves them feeling weak or like a failure and is to be disowned and avoided at all costs.

For some women, there is an intense fear that others will be overwhelmed by their needs and leave them or stop loving them. To avoid this, they try to be perfect inside and out. The strain is enormous.

Amy, a 17-year-old bulimic, recently began to see how this fear affected her life:

> *I know it sounds crazy and isn't logical, but I genuinely feel that to be loved, I must be perfect. If a guy doesn't like me, I'm sure it's because I'm not thin enough, or my hair isn't nice enough, or I'm not smart enough. Then I have to work out, study harder, look better. It never occurs to me to think, Do I like him? All I can think about is that I'm not good enough.*

The self-imposed demands of perfection and the fear of rejection that eating-disordered people experience interfere with the development of comfortable, intimate relationships. The dilemma is a difficult one. If someone can't reach out and allow herself to need someone else, to be vulnerable to someone else, how can she really get to know that person and let herself be known?

The Complete Picture

Because the symptoms of bingeing, vomiting, exercising, or starving can be so disruptive and frightening, it is easy to pay attention only to those behaviors. To do so, however, misses the point. The overt symptoms are just the tip of the iceberg. Beneath the surface lies a much larger piece of the picture—a complicated and complex world of feelings and experiences that are very much a part of the eating disorder. Both the visible and invisible parts need to be acknowledged in order to understand the disorders of bulimia nervosa, anorexia nervosa, and binge eating.

3

Rules and Relationships

The Family Context of Eating Disorders

When someone in a family develops an eating disorder, it is an opportunity to pay attention. Every family has its difficulties. Often it takes something going wrong to stop and evaluate what might need to change to better meet the needs of everyone involved.

No one knows for certain what aspects of family life contribute to a child developing an eating disorder. What is clear, however, is that once a family member does develop an eating disorder, that problem, in and of itself, generates stress for everyone and exacerbates whatever difficulties may have existed before. This, in turn, usually results in the maintenance or the increase of disordered eating.

With any eating disorder, the goal is to help that person take hold of her own life, so that she is making responsible choices about how to take care of her body and her emotions. It is not always clear how to help someone take care of herself. In some cases, this will mean more active support, limit setting, and structure. In other cases, it will mean backing off and letting go. Every family differs in terms of what is needed, and each family's situation will continually change over time.

Families with an eating-disordered child vary tremendously. In some families everything looks okay on the surface. In others the picture is overtly chaotic, with alcoholism, drug addiction, gambling, or family violence obvious to the onlooker.

However, in families in which there is an eating-disordered child, there is a common thread: the existing rules and practices that bind the family together are not accommodating the shifting needs of the individual members. The work in each family is to assess what is needed to help each person grow and change while maintaining the family connections.

What Are Family Rules?

In every family, rules evolve to help the family function. These rules have to do with how to live together, how to express intimacy, how to disagree, and how to express needs. Which feelings and behaviors are encouraged and which are disapproved of are also dictated by the rules of the family. These rules are an attempt to provide everyone with a sense of belonging, a means of communicating, and a way of living together on a day-to-day basis.

There are many examples of family rules. The following are some that you might be familiar with: "Fighting in this house is not allowed." "The family that eats together stays together." "There are no locked doors in this house."

These rules are attempts at handling disagreement, fostering closeness, and expressing togetherness. As children grow older, flexible rules allow them to enjoy more freedom as well as assume additional responsibility. Later curfews and more privacy, for example, are balanced with more household chores. Family rules exist for parents as well. In some families, these rules can provide parents the opportunity to have a life of their own, for example, closing bedroom doors at night or going out without their children. In other families, the rules that are established can inhibit parents' freedom, for example, bedroom doors are always open, and babysitters are never hired. Rules do not have to be spoken to be heard. Often they are conveyed via subtle messages that are adhered to as if they were carved in stone. A certain facial expression or physical posture can carry a great deal of meaning about what is or is not acceptable in a family.

When Rules Don't Work

In many families in which someone has developed an eating disorder, those rules that originally evolved to keep the family together end up inhibiting the growth and development of the individual members of the family—children and parents alike. This does not necessarily cause an eating disorder, but it very well may keep someone who is eating disordered from developing a healthy attitude toward both food and herself.

Parents are not ill-intentioned when conveying family rules. The rules that develop are an attempt to help the family cope and get along together. Parents tend to bring the rules they learned during their own upbringing into their new families, thus perpetuating patterns of coping and relating throughout the generations. This transmission of patterns, however, can perpetuate less-than-ideal rules and practices.

Janie, 18, a recovered anorexic, recalled her surprise when she noticed that her grandmother treated her mother in the same way her mother treated her:

> *When we all went to visit Grandma for Christmas, her first words to my mother were, "Isn't that a bit too much makeup for you?" I'm sure this has always been going on, but I had never noticed it. My mother's face flashed anger and disappointment. I wondered if my mother realized that scene could just as easily have been of her talking to me.*

In Janie's family and in the family her mother came from, one rule that was apparent was that looks are important. Another rule, or pattern of relating, was that one person had a right to comment on someone else's looks or behaviors regardless of the person's age. In both families, however, the rules resulted in an accentuated focus on looks, a feeling of being criticized, and an undermining of each person's ability to decide for herself how she should look or dress.

In both families, these rules needed to be reevaluated, but it wasn't until Janie became anorexic and therapy was started that anyone imagined the family rules were keeping Janie dependent upon her mother's opinions to decide how she should look or feel.

Sometimes rules don't work because parents disagree about what the rules should be. The child does not get a clear message about what behavior is expected from her.

Betty, the young woman we mentioned earlier who used men and food for security, spoke to us about what it was like when her parents disagreed:

> *My parents could never agree about anything. My mother's story went back to when I was a baby. She felt it was important I be on a schedule— that I slept from 7:00 p.m. to 7:00 a.m., and that I ate at the same times*

every day. She said she would have had me trained at three months, but my father disagreed. He thought I could go to sleep easily if I were just held for a few minutes. He didn't understand how my mother could let me cry for such a long time. She would feel I was being manipulative, and he was supporting that and going against her. My father felt my mother was cold and unfeeling. That fight in some form or other went on all my life.

It took looking at their different ways of acting to realize that only two things made me feel good—one was food and the other was a man. My father was kind and comforting to me, but it would come at a big price. Whenever he took my side, my mother would stop speaking to me. So as a kid, I ate. I do the same thing now that I am older. I can only stop bingeing if I'm with a man.

One of the most common ways rules don't work has to do with parents' approaches to the eating disorder itself. Each parent brings to the situation rules he or she believes will stop the eating disorder. Often those rules differ, and that's when trouble can occur. One of the most crucial aspects in dealing with an eating disorder is for parents to act together in their strategy toward their child and not be in conflict with one another.

Eileen, a 25-year-old recovered anorexic, describes her situation this way:

When I became anorexic, my father kept saying, "I don't know what's wrong with you—just eat a pastrami sandwich, and everything will be all right. You look terrible—your arms and legs are sticks, and all your clothes hang off of you."

My mother would disagree. She'd say, "Eileen must be feeling badly.

You can't make her eat. We need to find out what's going on inside of her.
Just making her eat won't solve anything."
   My father definitely did not buy that. He thought I just needed to be
forced to eat. So they fought, and I starved.

When someone develops a symptom such as an eating disorder, it is
that person's own way of fighting to evoke change. The person, however, is not someone who can fight openly; she is not a rebel. Thus
her fight is subtle and disguised. When the family can understand
an eating disorder as a sign to question family rules and patterns, or
parental communications, the other problems have hope of resolution.
Families that can adapt to the changing needs of their family members
by reevaluating the rules (or couples who can come to an agreement
regarding the couple's rules) have a better chance of the eating disorder taking a transient, short-lived course as opposed to becoming
embedded in both the individual's and the family's life.

When Rules Affect Feelings

Pearl Greene, the mother of an anorexic daughter, was an eight-year-old
child when her own mother developed cancer. Her mother spent many
years bedridden as Pearl, the only daughter, tended to her. Pearl's childhood was lost to her mother's illness, and as Pearl entered her teenage
years without the freedom to date or enjoy after-school activities like
the other teenagers, her anger and resentment understandably grew. At
night, alone in bed and tearful, Pearl would wish that her mother would
die so she could have her own life. When Pearl was 15, her "wish"
was granted—but horror, not relief, followed. Maybe her mother had
known of Pearl's anger. Maybe it had killed her. Pearl's mother's death

did not release her; instead, it haunted her even through her own marriage and family life. In the Greene family, Pearl made it clear that anger was to be avoided at all cost.

Pearl's experience with death and her fear of the consequences of anger pervaded her experiences with others. The effects of Pearl's experience influenced her daughter, Emily, a 16-year-old high school student who is now recovering from anorexia nervosa. Emily describes it this way:

> *Whenever I would get angry at my father and start to say anything, my mother would put her hand over her heart like she was warning me. This would stop me cold. I'd just stop what I was saying and leave. But I always felt angry and frustrated. The first time my mother didn't do that was when I was in the hospital, and my parents thought I might die because I was so thin. Then my mother was more frightened about my dying than my getting angry.*

When family rules inhibit the experience or expression of feelings, the opportunities to accept and resolve these feelings are thwarted. Pent-up feelings may result in explosive episodes, in which release comes in a torrent of emotions that are uncontrollable and usually not productive. They can also exacerbate physical illnesses, including stomach problems, back pain, colitis, and asthma, or they may lead to psychological symptoms as expressed in an eating disorder. When symptoms are the result of unexpressed feelings, one not only misses the chance to learn how to accept emotions and use them constructively but can continue believing that everyone will respond to feelings like people at home did. Rules about feelings can be problematic in any family. When there is an eating disorder, rules about feelings can directly affect eating behaviors. In attempts to suppress or express feelings, eating and starving are easy substitutions. Even if it looks like nothing else is going on, if someone is bingeing or starving, it is critical to ask What would someone be thinking about or feeling if disordered eating weren't in the picture?

Areas of common trouble include the following.

Expression of Feelings:
"You're Going to Kill Your Father if You Say That"

In the Greene family, Pearl had made it clear that anger was to be avoided. This was not an arbitrary rule but an attempt on Pearl's part to keep the family together. From her own experience, she learned that anger was a powerful and dangerous emotion. The "rule" to not get angry was her way to avoid replicating in her new family what she believed happened in her family of origin. The problem with this rule was that, while it was well intentioned, it left all the members of the family restricted in their expression of a wide range of feelings.

The direct experience and expression of intense feelings such as anger, resentment, disappointment, jealousy, sadness, and loss are necessary for healthy functioning. In many eating-disordered families there is a rule, sometimes subtle, sometimes not, that these unpleasant feelings are to be avoided. Pearl thought anger could be hurtful. Others may have come from families in which feelings actually did get out of control and resulted in violence. Certainly, rules inhibiting emotional expression would feel like life-protecting devices in this case. For some people, expressing painful feelings is a sign of weakness. In any of these situations, when rules develop that stop the natural expression of feelings, finding effective and modulated means of expressing them may seem impossible.

Kevin Dwyer, 42, had grown up in a strict Irish Catholic family. In his family, one unquestioningly respected one's elders. Most displays of emotion were strongly discouraged. His own upbringing influenced how he raised his daughter Maureen. Maureen describes it this way:

My mother died when I was 6 years old, and my father remarried when I was 10. As soon as he married my stepmother, they both insisted I call her Mom. I didn't want to, but they forced me to. All the pictures of my mother were taken off the living room walls. I didn't mind that so much, but then my father made me put away all the pictures of my mother that I had in my bedroom. I'd have to sneak away to look at them. Sometimes I'd ask questions about my mother, and my father would give me a dirty look and say, "You only have one mother, ask her." When I got older, I really wanted to know things about her, particularly in what ways I was like her. But my father would never tell me. I had a ritual in those days. I would buy lots of sweets and gather all the pictures I had of my mother, close my bedroom door, eat, and look at them.

Kevin Dwyer was not trying to be mean to his daughter. It was just that he himself had never expressed his own feelings of sadness and loss as a child. Now as an adult, faced with the traumatic loss of his wife, he turned to the familiar rules of his family: "Pull it together," "Don't think about it," and certainly "Don't let it show."

Naturally, Maureen abided by these same unspoken rules, and food became the only safe outlet for her unexpressed feelings about her mother. Eating helped her to ease her loneliness and sadness.

Expression of Conflict: "Our Family Never Fights"

One of the reasons that families avoid direct expression of intense feelings is that they fear conflict among family members. If people say what they feel, they may not agree with each other, and tension, arguing, and conflict will result. To some, conflict calls into question the family's closeness; it is interpreted to mean that people do not love one another. Complaining or disagreeing threatens the bonds of the family. Therefore, a high value is placed on everyone getting along well. The rule, then, often unspoken, is that one doesn't behave in ways that may cause conflict.

Such a rule, designed to keep the family close, may have consequences for the children. When there is no acceptable way to disagree and be different, there is no way for someone to learn to trust and value her own experiences.

Katherine, 18, once 82 pounds, has been in therapy for three years and is now at a normal weight. She describes a history typical of many anorexics:

> I was always the good one around the house. My room was never messy. I did well in school. I always helped my mother. I know my parents hated fighting. If my brother or I ever raised our voices, my mother would tell us, "Shh; now, say it in a nice tone." How can you be angry in a nice tone?
>
> I went on being the good child and the good student. I never disobeyed.
>
> It was in my sophomore year in high school that I began dieting after gaining weight during the summer. Dieting and losing weight was a real high for me. After I'd lost a lot of weight, my mother got upset and tried to make me eat. But she couldn't.
>
> I didn't know it then, but now I realize that my not eating made me powerful. It was really a way to finally do what I wanted instead of pleasing everyone else.

The reasons to avoid fighting were different for Joan and Jim Ross. Jim grew up watching his father and older brother fight constantly. Often the fighting got out of control, and on one occasion Jim's father knocked Jim's brother unconscious. Another time, Jim's brother was so mad that he threatened to kill everyone in the house. Jim, at age 10, believed he might do it. Jim grew up fearful that anger could be dangerous. When he married Joan and had children, his feelings about conflict didn't change.

Joan had reasons of her own for wanting a peaceful household. Joan's parents never fought. They prided themselves on this quality and taught Joan that a couple with a good marriage didn't disagree. In the Ross family the rule "no disagreements" was strictly adhered to.

For Pam, the Rosses' bulimic 17-year-old daughter, this presented an agonizing dilemma. At an eating-disorder group, she asked:

> *What can I do? It's a losing battle. All my friends stay out and go to parties. I want to be a part of it, but my folks get upset. They want me to be home early and always stick around for Sunday—Family Day, they call it. They have this idea that we're all supposed to be so close. I love my parents, but sometimes what they want is too much. Whenever I get pissed off at them and their ridiculous ideas, they get incredibly upset. My mother cries; my father looks hurt and says, "Let's just forget all this and have a nice evening." I want to scream—but what I do instead is eat. It's the only thing that keeps me from fighting with them—and fighting is just too upsetting. I'm so miserable about this whole thing.*

As Pam's eating disorder increased, the family became more and more embroiled in her problem. However, as the focus shifted to food, Pam's struggle to disagree with her parents was obscured. Little by little Pam stopped fighting with her parents about going out. As long as the struggle remained in the arena of eating, there was less and less hope of resolution of the other issues regarding her attempts to grow up.

Assuming and Ascribing Feelings: "You Must Be Hungry"

When open communication is inhibited, family members are left to guess or assume what the others feel. When assumptions about feelings are made, children grow up without the opportunity to learn about, trust, and communicate their own feelings.

Elaine Peters, now 42, came from a family in which every birthday and holiday were celebrated. Forgetting family members' birthdays meant you weren't thinking about them either because you were angry at them or they didn't mean much to you. If someone forgot Elaine's birthday, she was hurt, and her family accepted her feelings as legitimate.

Her husband, Richard, 44, on the other hand, came from a family that rarely celebrated birthdays or made much of holidays. In his family, the "rule" was to buy a gift for someone when one felt like buying something or when one saw something special that someone else would want. His family believed birthdays were artificially imposed occasions that did not warrant special attention or gift buying.

The first year that they were married, Elaine's birthday came and went without Richard saying a thing. Elaine was hurt and upset. To her, Richard's behavior meant that she was forgotten and unloved. She responded to Richard with angry silence. Richard, on the other hand, did not know why Elaine was treating him this way, and he responded by emotionally withdrawing. His withdrawal was further proof to Elaine that he didn't care enough about her, and their frustrating interaction continued.

Neither Elaine nor Richard asked what the other was feeling. Elaine assumed she knew what Richard's behavior meant because of what it would have meant in her own family. Richard didn't ask because in his family it was considered pushy to ask people what they felt—if they wanted you to know, they'd tell you. By operating under rules that they were accustomed to in their own families, Elaine and Richard could only see the situation as their original families would have seen it. Each was stuck in his or her own perspective, so they could not move on to develop new rules that would be more satisfying for both of them. The birthday situation finally erupted into an angry fight. The fight ended when Richard resolved to remember all future holidays and birthdays. However, while the gift-giving aspect of the problem was solved, both Richard and Elaine continued to avoid asking what the other person was feeling. A pattern of guessing or assuming rather than asking about what someone was feeling persisted as a family norm—and often one or the other was wrong.

In families where feelings are not directly expressed but instead assumed, the die is cast for children who enter into these families. They, too, have feelings ascribed to them that they don't necessarily experience.

Kerry, 22 and bulimic, brought this issue up in her support group:

> *My parents spent my childhood telling me what they thought I was feeling instead of ever asking. They weren't trying to be mean or anything. It's just that they'd say things like, "It's 42 degrees. You must be cold," or "You don't mind when we ask you to babysit for your brother, right?," or "I know you must be hungry." I'd always know from their questions what they'd want me to say, and I'd answer that way—I hated to let them down. I also think I believed that they really knew what I wanted better than I did. Even today I expect people will know what I want without my having to say so. It's ironic—now when people ask me what I feel or want, I resent their not knowing.*

Kerry was responded to with much head nodding in the group. "I've been talking a lot about this in therapy," a 24-year-old bulimic woman said:

> I too was raised by parents who always thought they knew what I was thinking. I was a quiet kid, and I remember if I wasn't bubbly and talkative about guys and school (like my sister Chrissie), my mother would think I was mad at her. "What are you so angry at?" she'd ask. "What did I do now?" Then I would get mad at her because her questions were so annoying. She made me wonder if I was angry at her when I was quiet. It got so that at times I didn't know what I was feeling. Even now, my insides seem like a puzzle—sometimes I can't figure out what it is I'm feeling. I know my mother didn't mean to be cruel, but the effect was cruel. I've ended up so unsure of myself.

Growing up in a family where feelings are inhibited instead of openly expressed can lead to assuming and ascribing feelings in later relationships. Lila, a 24-year-old laxative abuser, talked about how this was so in her marriage to Charles, 29:

> When I was growing up, no one in my family would ever say if he or she felt angry. If I even got mildly angry about something, my folks would get upset. They feared my being angry meant that they weren't being good parents. When I got angry, I'd end up feeling guilty. I learned to act as though I felt fine no matter what was going on inside me.
>
> Now, as an adult, I don't even know if I'm angry half the time—and if I am, I certainly can't say it.
>
> After I started therapy for the eating disorder, though, my therapist helped me see that at times I do get angry at Charles. But instead of telling him that I'm mad, I'll think he's the one who's upset, and I'll ask him,

"What's wrong?" He'll say nothing. Then I keep asking him over and over what he's upset about. Pretty soon, he is angry at me because I'm bugging him so much.

My therapist helped me see that the way I let out my own feelings is by putting them on Charles. Now, whenever I think he's angry at me, I ask myself whether that's what I'm feeling.

Every family has its share of miscommunications and misunderstandings. It is unclear whether problems with feelings actually cause an eating disorder. But once an eating disorder is in the picture, it is very clear that problems with feelings can keep someone from knowing what to do instead of eating or starving. Finding the tools to know what is going on inside is always a critical part of the work toward recovery.

When Rules Don't Shift: Problems Growing Up

Another common problem in families is that rules do not flexibly shift in response to family members' ages, needs, and capabilities. For children, in particular, flexible rules are necessary to allow for natural dependence while encouraging increasing autonomy. This enables children to test their expanding capacities in a safe environment that allows for failure while parents are still available to help.

The transition from being the parents of young children, where watchfulness and protectiveness are necessary for the child's survival, to being the parents of adolescents, where this watchfulness should decrease, is a difficult one for many families. It is a shift that requires parents to allow the teenager to try things on her own even when the parents know a better way. When parents are able to make this shift, the children develop an increasing sense of their own competency and ability to negotiate the demands of the outside world. When parents have difficulty shifting rules, when they disagree about what the rules should be, or when rigid and fixed rules do not allow for independent behavior, children may fight for these changes in indirect ways. Withdrawal from the family, the use of drugs or alcohol, and the refusal to eat or eating secretly are among the behaviors resorted to when a child feels helpless and controlled.

While these behaviors may allow for a feeling of independence, they do so at a high cost. They limit the child's natural and healthy capacities to grow up and achieve a life independent of her parents, and instead leave her with a destructive method of asserting herself.

When Rules Inhibit Freedom

Jeanette Cuso was 16 when her mother brought her into therapy for bulimia. "She just binges all night long," her mother said. "I buy food for the family, and it's gone by morning. Then she's in the bathroom at all hours of the night getting rid of it."

Jeanette saw the problem differently. "That may be what's upsetting you," she told her mother, "but I'm suffocating. You never let me stay out with my friends. I have to be in at 10:00 p.m. on weekends. All my friends stay out later. I'm always the one who has to leave the parties. You don't trust me, but you've never given me a chance."

The rules were no different for Jeanette than for her younger 14-year-old sister. Being older made no difference.

The Cusos, first-generation Italian Americans, were fearful of what problems freedom could bring to teenagers. Drugs were rampant in Jeanette's school, and one of her friends had already had an abortion. The Cusos were not going to let that happen to Jeanette. But Jeanette did not feel protected by her parents' rules. The only thing she felt was that she was being punished—and for no reason. At night, while she sat at home, feeling lonely and resentful, the frustration was overwhelming. Eating and purging allowed her to calm her feelings, but at the cost of finding more appropriate ways of developing her independence and taking hold of her life.

When Boundaries and Privacy Are Sacrificed

All families create boundaries to allow for privacy, independence, increased control, and a sense of separateness. Just as people create boundaries around the land they own so no one will trespass, so are there boundaries around people. There are individual boundaries for each person and boundaries around groups of people, such as with spouses and siblings.

When the family has difficulty establishing, maintaining, and respecting boundaries, problems develop. People can feel intruded upon. The most extreme boundary violation is incest, where a child's own body is not safe from intrusion. A less extreme occurrence is when a parent enters a teenager's room without permission and goes through her possessions or reads her private diary. Boundaries, especially those that have to do with privacy, also need to shift as children grow up.

Boundaries in families with eating disorders may be blurred. There may not be sufficient privacy, and closed doors may not be respected or even exist. In one family we met at a support group, all the doors had been removed from the children's rooms.

The intrusion may be emotional and not easy to pinpoint. As we saw in families where feelings are ascribed and not expressed, a child may not learn to be comfortable as an individual separate from her parents, with different ideas, thoughts, and feelings.

Marcia, a 24-year-old who suffered from anorexia nervosa, talked about living in her family:

I always felt confused when I was growing up. My mother would use the word we whether she was talking about me or about herself. Someone would ask how I was, and she would say, "We're fine." I had trouble figuring out what were my feelings and what were hers.

One of the ways in which parents set a boundary between themselves and their children is by establishing rules. When parents make rules, they are assuming a position of authority and creating a structure in the family that permits children to feel protected and independent.

For some parents, the position of authority is difficult to assume. They want to feel close to their children and fear that if they set limits, their children will get angry and not love them. This type of closeness can make it hard for the child to become independent. If a child is made to feel like the friend of a parent, rather than the child, she does not have the opportunity to separate from the family and develop meaningful relationships apart from the parents.

Rachel, 24, and her mother, Elise, were best friends. They spent lots of time together and told each other everything. Rachel felt lucky to have a mother who was so much fun. It was only with her mother that her excessive weight did not make her feel uncomfortable about herself.

The trouble came when Rachel met a man she liked. She had rarely dated during college, but now there was Richard, someone who was also interested in her. As Rachel and Richard began to spend time together, Rachel noticed she didn't feel like calling her mother every day.

When Rachel didn't call Elise, Elise would call and complain to Rachel about her loneliness and ask if Rachel had forgotten she had a mother. Rachel would then insist to Richard that her mother come with them on different weekend outings. Richard resented this, and it led to many arguments between them.

After a few months of this, Richard ended the relationship. He was tired of having Rachel's mother so much a part of their relationship. Rachel, upset and torn between closeness to her mother and her relationship with Richard, contacted us for therapy.

Rachel realized she and her mother were and had always been too close. There were insufficient boundaries between mother and daughter. Rachel was having trouble developing a private, independent life without feeling as though she were deserting her mother. She was beginning to suspect that her extra pounds kept her closer to home.

Boundary violations can appear in many forms. They can be subtle, such as speaking for someone else, or more problematic, such as reading someone else's mail. The worst possible sort of boundary violation with the worst consequences for the victim is incest. Reports of sexual abuse and incest within the eating-disordered population vary tremendously. Research indicates that anywhere from 4 to 65 percent of patients have been sexually abused.[12]

After two years in therapy, Denise, 26 and a binge eater, opened up about the abuse she suffered as a child:

> *At night I'd listen for his footsteps. The house would be quiet. I'd hear the whir of the refrigerator, the hiss of the steam—and then his footsteps. He'd tell me to shove over in bed, he wanted to hold me. But he never stopped there. He said my skin was soft, I was pretty. He made me touch him. But for some reason the part that was the worst was when he kissed me. Everything else I could pretend wasn't happening to me. But the taste of his saliva, the smell of his breath, that part I could never block out.*

When Denise's father left her room, Denise would retreat to the safety of the kitchen. There she crammed food into her mouth quickly to rid herself of the tastes in her mouth.

> *I felt safe then. The food numbed everything. It was a wall around me that made me feel like nothing, no one could get in. Weight became a wall too. Sixty extra pounds of fat is a hard thing to penetrate. Sometimes I imagine I'm this little person inside my big shell of a body.*

Without the physical and psychological boundaries between father and daughter that should normally exist in a family to protect a child, and without her mother's help to enforce these boundaries, Denise had to resort to food and weight to obliterate the horrifying experiences her father subjected her to. The type of trauma that Denise experienced is often never revealed. Physical violations such as incest leave the victim with a sense of powerlessness that pervades her experiences with people for the rest of her life and often contributes to substance abuse, such as eating disorders, in an attempt to block out and deny the impact of these traumas.

When Rules Are Unpredictable: Chaotic Families

In some families, difficulties arise because the rules are changeable, confusing, and unpredictable. As a result, the child learns to depend on herself, not on the stability of the family, and independence may come too soon, leaving the child fearful and anxious. She may turn to food to calm her anxiety or refuse it to make herself feel stronger.

In families where the rules are chaotic or unstable, drug or alcohol abuse may be part of the family picture. When parents are involved with alcohol or drugs, they cannot provide a stable family structure and consistent rules for the child. These families often function from crisis to crisis. The household can be disorganized, and many times the children are left with responsibilities that would otherwise be in the hands of the parents. A child or adolescent in such a position is left feeling inadequate. She does not have the resources or abilities to cope with all the problems that occur in filling the gaps. While she may appear to be functioning well, this is often a precocious independence and an autonomy built on sand.

It took Grace, 15, months to speak to her support group about her divorced mother's drinking problem:

> *I don't know what it's going to be like when I come home from school. If she's had a "good" day, she's a lot of fun. She'll ask me how my day was, she'll suggest we make dinner together or go shopping. But if she's been drinking (which lately is more often than not), she'll have passed out on the couch with the TV blaring. Then I know if I don't shop for dinner and cook, my two younger brothers and I won't eat. Even when she wakes up, she's so groggy that it's up to me to get my brothers to do homework and get to bed. At around 11:00 p.m., the house is quiet, and I can finally get to my homework. I'm just scared I can't keep it up. Last week I got my first C ever. This is getting to me.*

What Grace didn't tell the group until two months later was how food fit in.

> *At night when it's quiet, when I'm doing my homework, I eat. All night sometimes. But I'm scared of gaining weight, so that's why I started taking laxatives. It started at one or two, but now I can take 50 at a time before they work.*

When substance abuse exists among parents, strong messages are communicated about experiencing and conveying feelings—in particular, that you can numb your feelings and that pain or upset will not go away on its own. The children hear a clear message: feelings are unmanageable, and substances help.

When Rules Focus on Appearance

In many families in which eating disorders occur, there is a very high value placed on appearance. Rules about how one looks are as powerful as rules about how one behaves. This doesn't mean that paying attention to looks and health can cause an eating disorder. In fact, if a parent diets or watches his or her weight, this will not necessarily result in an eating-disordered child. However, constant self-deprecating remarks about bulging thighs or repeated talk about the need to lose weight can send the message that thinness is to be prized above all else. If attention to looks is an ongoing and much discussed concern in the family, then pressure to maintain perfection can prevail, and disordered eating and body image can result.[13]

In that regard, in some families, looking good is synonymous with being worthwhile. Audrey, 24 and bulimic, described it this way:

When I walk in the door to greet my parents, the first thing they say is, "Oh, you look great—you've lost a few pounds" or "Did you cut your hair? It looks shorter." The worst thing is when they won't say anything. Then I know that they think I've gained weight or don't look so good, and they don't want to hurt my feelings. It's ridiculous, but now if someone I'm with doesn't say I look good, I think they're being critical of me.

No question commenting on looks is part of our culture, particularly among women. "You look so good! Did you lose weight?" often replaces "hello" when two women meet. In families, the question is not whether looks are noticed, but whether a focus on looks supersedes attention to other aspects of who the person is.

Often parents may not be aware of the stringent messages they are giving about food, weight, and self-control. A father was surprised that his 25-year-old daughter was bulimic. When asked about his own food habits, he said, "I do worry about my weight. I've trained myself over the years not to eat many sweets. Every night I eat half an oatmeal cookie. If it's a whole cookie, I cut it in half and wrap the other half in Saran Wrap to eat the next night. I never eat more than that half a cookie, no matter what the occasion."

His daughter could not help but criticize herself for her own lack of self-discipline. If she ate one bite more than she wanted to, she felt compelled to vomit everything she had just eaten.

Karen, a 17-year-old anorexic, spoke about her mother's preoccupation with appearance:

> *My mother was always talking about weight. She was on a new diet every other week. She would be at my father to lose weight. She'd keep at him until he would go to Weight Watchers. Then the two of them would be watching everything they ate and what I ate. My mother would say, "All anyone in this family has to do is look at food, and they gain weight."*
>
> *I recall when my brother's fiancée broke off their engagement. He was really upset, and he started eating a lot. Soon he had a potbelly. Whenever my mother would see him, she'd tell him how awful he looked. She never asked him how he felt. I could see my brother feeling worse when he spent any time with my parents.*

My mother would comment about every pound I gained. My junior year in high school, she became even more concerned about my weight. She warned me about what happens to freshman girls in college. She said I should be 10 pounds lighter than my usual weight, so when I gained the 10 pounds in college, I wouldn't have that college freshman look. There wasn't a day I walked in the house from school that she didn't comment on how I dressed and what I looked like.

What she said about gaining weight in college really scared me. I remember starting to diet, thinking I'd get a head start before I went to college. The more weight I took off, the better I felt. My mother thought so too. It got so that I was afraid that if I ate anything, I'd gain weight. It was only when I started to faint that my mother realized my looking good might kill me.

Karen's mother was not ill-intentioned. She was only transmitting the rules about appearance that she had grown up with. She herself was an attractive woman, and her attractiveness was a quality for which she was often praised and admired. Her focus on looks was not meant to hurt Karen but was an attempt at encouraging a quality that she thought would be helpful to her daughter.

Another reason why appearance is so highly valued in some families is that some parents feel responsible for how their child looks or behaves, responsible in a way that overrides the child's right to determine how she feels she should look or act. Consider, for example, the child who has a messy room. Some parents feel it is a negative reflection of their parenting if their child doesn't take good care of her room. The same is often the case with the child's body. In some families a messy or overweight child is seen as a sign that something is wrong with the parents; therefore, every effort is made to urge the child to lose weight. In these cases, however, the goal in mind is not merely to protect the child, but to reduce the uneasiness the parents feel about themselves.

Changing the Rules

When someone in a family or relationship develops an eating disorder, it is important to evaluate unspoken rules in one's interactions and to question how they may need fine-tuning. For some, this will mean changing so that the person with an eating disorder is less dependent on others. Sometimes, though, it may mean that parents take more control and assert more authority, both with the food and in other arenas. In the following chapters, we will tell you how to get support in evaluating what is needed and how to make these changes. No matter what your situation, you can immediately start to help by thinking about what rules work—and what rules don't—in your relationship. Examining unspoken rules is a critical and ongoing part of setting the stage for recovery.

Part II

Confronting
the Problem

4

No More Secrets

Bringing It Out in the Open

If you suspect or know that someone is eating disordered, one of the first questions you will probably ask yourself is whether you should say anything to the person you're worried about. And if you do speak to her, what should you say?

If you think someone is eating disordered, this is no time for secrets. If the person does not know you are worried about her, the first thing you must do is tell her. Silence at these times will at best continue the discomfort and at worst lead to a dangerous and serious problem being ignored. No change can occur without first breaking the silence. Remember, if the unspoken rule in your house is not to say anything that will make someone uncomfortable, it is time right now to start changing the rules.

Planning to Talk

Bringing up the subject of an eating disorder is never an easy task, but if done with some planning and forethought, difficulties and embarrassments can be minimized. What you say can potentially influence the course of the person's recovery. You will need to anticipate how you should approach the subject, what will be said, and who will say it.

This chapter will help you anticipate what will happen in the discussion and will offer effective guidelines. By planning the discussion in advance, you can ease the discomfort and anxiety you are inevitably feeling, and, by being prepared, you will have the best chance of being understood.

How to Approach the Problem

Use the following guidelines before speaking with the person you're concerned about.

1. *Think through who the best person is to do the talking.*
   If you are a parent, decide with your husband or wife if you should both be there, or if a one-on-one conversation would work better. If the latter is the case, decide who would have an easier time talking to her without getting upset. Don't involve the rest of the family until after your child is spoken with privately.
   If you are a sibling and concerned about your sister, you may want to speak with her privately, or you may want your parents to do so. If your sister is a minor or you are a minor, your parents must be informed.
   If you are a spouse, it is your responsibility to speak with your wife

or husband. You can discuss together if anyone else needs to be told. Respect her privacy, and do not speak with friends, in-laws, or others until you speak with your spouse.

If you are a friend or roommate, you should be the person to do the talking initially. Do not go to authorities or family until you have spoken with your friend first. In a house in which there are several roommates, a house meeting can be called in which anyone affected by the problem can participate. In the latter case, only one person should initiate the discussion, so that there will be less likelihood of the person feeling attacked by everyone at once.

2. *Pick a time to talk when you are feeling calm.* Do not try to bring up this subject when you are angry, upset, or hurt. If you are upset, your pain may be burdensome to the other person—it may be harder for her to open up if she fears causing you even more pain. In addition, your feelings may interfere with your achieving the goals that you have in mind. Do not bring up your concerns in the middle of a fight. Accusations, confrontations, and pleas to change will only result in shutting down potential lines of communication. The other person is likely to end up defending herself and will perceive your concerns as a criticism or an attack. If someone is defensive, she certainly will not be open to hearing you out at that time.

3. *Pick a time to talk when you know you won't be interrupted.* For example, don't start such a discussion 10 minutes before you have to go to work, or you will feel very pressured. This pressure can make things go badly. The time limit may discourage the other person from opening up to you because of a fear of being cut off. Both of you must know you have as much time as is needed to talk.

4. *Consider writing down what you want to say ahead of time.* It is inevitable that you will feel anxious or worried when you start to talk;

that is natural and to be expected. By familiarizing yourself with what you want to say before you actually say it, you will be clearer when you do speak, and your anxiety may be lessened. You'll also be sure to remember everything you want to say once you start talking. There are three things you will need to address in the discussion: what your worries are, how you feel, and what you would like the outcome of the discussion to be.

What Is Worrying You?

When you discuss your concerns, you need to explain why you have come to suspect a problem. You will want to be specific about what you see with regard to the eating, purging, exercising, starving, or weight-related behaviors. If you have noticed changes that affect your relationship, you will need to point these out as well. Use the information from the checklists in Chapter 1 to help you clarify what it is you see or suspect.

When you have the discussion, you are going to have to be as direct and frank as you can. For example, as hard as it is to say, "I hear you vomiting," this is much more honest than "I think you spend a lot of time in the bathroom." If you say the latter, you are leaving the door open for the problem to get ignored or denied. The implied message is "I really don't want to talk about this either." If you are open in your approach, you are saying, "I know this is embarrassing, but I want to be of help. Let's address this problem head-on for what it is."

You are going to have to be careful not to make this an indictment of what you see. Your observations should not be listed as evidence of wrongdoing, but should be discussed gently as bases for your concern. This is a subtle distinction that has to do with tone and approach but one that can make all the difference in the world.

During your talk you will have to stick to the issue and keep yourself from becoming distracted. If she changes the subject, tell her you'd like to find some time to speak about these other matters, but for now you don't want to avoid the problem at hand. You should let her know that *you* know this is a hard problem to discuss, but that you don't want to let the issue get sidetracked.

What Do You Feel About It?

When planning what you will say, include letting the person know what your experience is. One way to do this is to use what are called "I" statements. "I" statements are statements that focus on your own feelings and experience, not that of the other person.

Merely using the word *I* does not make for an "I" statement. "I think there's something wrong with you" and "What is the matter with you? I wonder what kind of person eats all that food and then throws up?" are *not* "I" statements. They focus on the other person and will be heard as attacking or blaming.

An "I" statement involves talking about yourself: "I've been worried about what I'm seeing. I haven't known whether to approach you or not, but I'm feeling too troubled not to say something," or "The missing food is making me really angry. I don't like walking around being so mad at you. I want to find some way of working this out."

We are not suggesting you negate your own anger, frustration, or hurt. You are in an upsetting situation and will naturally have many reactions to this. However, merely venting feelings will only result in the person's becoming defensive and your being shut out. We are encouraging you to express your feelings in a way that you will be heard.

Using "I" statements does not mean you can't talk about the other person. Of course you will need to tell her why you are worried and what you perceive the problem to be. ("I've heard you vomiting," or "You keep mentioning how worried you are about your weight lately.") But it is important to avoid telling the person how you think *she* feels. For example, avoid making statements like "You must be very angry, or you wouldn't be doing this." Resist judging the other person's experience. This will decrease the possibility of the other person's feeling attacked or controlled and will increase the success of your conversation.

What Are Your Goals?

The third area that you should think through is what you would like to accomplish in this discussion. Be sure your goals are realistic and attainable.

Impossible Goals

If your goal in approaching someone is to get her to stop bingeing, purging, or starving—STOP! While down the line, you may well want to set limits or take charge (such as with an anorexic or severely bulimic teenager), it would be premature to do so at this first stage. This is an impossible task, and you will fail in your attempts. Indeed, if you are coercive, you may unwittingly encourage her to be more secretive and less talkative. You will most likely end up in a control battle and make matters worse. For any eating-disordered person, bringing the problem out in the open is a beginning stage in the process of recovery. The first goals have to be clear, small, and contained.

Realistic Goals

Opening the Doors to Talk

You will want to let her know that she can talk with you and that you're interested in helping her. If, in your family or relationship, people tend not to open up to each other, you may need to make a special point of your availability to listen, to help, and even to make changes.

Changing How the Eating Disorder Is Affecting You

A realistic goal can be to change how the eating problem is interfering with your life or your relationship with her. For example, if someone you love is losing a lot of weight or vomiting after meals, inevitably you will be worried, angry, or frightened. One thing to consider is whether you are the only one thinking that a problem exists, or if the other person is worried too. You may want to try and understand how the other person sees her eating behaviors and to find out what she is doing about it.

More specific goals may have to do with how the eating behavior affects the household. Roommates talk to us about the frustration of food missing from the kitchen. Siblings are angry that there is vomit on the toilet. Parents consistently talk about their daughter's belligerent or depressed attitude when food is around—mealtimes have devolved into stressful battlegrounds. In these cases, it's best to change the way food is handled in your household.

In any of these situations, do not expect that the goals will be accomplished right away. It is very important to take small steps and not focus too far ahead. For now, all you want to do is think about what needs to change. For example, if you need to discuss how food is handled in the house, don't try to work it out immediately. Set up another time to do this. Everything does not have to be worked out in one discussion. If the other person isn't worried about the eating problems that you see, don't try to argue with her. The first step is just to listen and try to understand how she sees things. Only once you know what is already being done can you proceed to the next step of figuring out whether more help is needed.

Helping Her Get the Help She Needs

Sometimes, it will turn out that the person already knows there is a problem and has sought help herself. This might be the case when you are talking with a friend or spouse. Then the goal would be to figure out whether you can be of support in any way.

However, often the person may deny that anything is wrong. When this is the case, the most important goal would be to help her get an evaluation to determine if a problem exists and, if so, what needs to be done next. In this situation, tell her that maybe nothing is wrong, but if indeed there is a problem, you don't want to look back in a couple of years and feel like you have missed her completely. Offer your help in finding a suitable professional who can do an evaluation. If you are the parent of a child or adolescent, you will have to do the work to arrange for a treatment consultation. Your daughter should know that the family will be seeking help so that she can begin to eat normally again. (Chapter 6 will discuss at length the resources available to both you and the sufferer.)

Giving It Your Best Shot

1. *You can practice the discussion with someone.* This may seem unnecessary, but it is surprising how many people enter into very serious

conversations without really thinking through what they want to say or what might go wrong. Anticipating the talk will certainly help to avert a disastrous interaction. If there is a family member or friend who is aware of the eating problem, you can practice what you'd like to say before you actually speak with the eating-disordered person herself. Tell that person what it is you want to say. Ask him or her to respond by saying the type of things you are worried your daughter, spouse, or friend will say. This way, you'll have had time to anticipate some of the difficult spots, and when the real situation occurs, you'll be more prepared to handle it. If there is no one else who is aware of the problem, respect the other person's privacy. A support group is a good place to practice what you would like to say. In these groups, confidentiality and the anonymity of the eating-disordered person can be maintained. (See Chapter 6 for more information on support groups.)

2. *You can stop the conversation before it gets out of control.* Keep this in mind when thinking about what you will say. This discussion is most likely going to be difficult and, if you are not careful, can lead to a battle of wills. Remember, it will be up to you to keep the conversation from becoming a fight, no matter what the reaction of the other person is. Let your concern show. If you find, though, in the discussion that you become angry or upset, STOP THE CONVERSATION before it gets heated and hurtful. You should tell the person that you want to continue talking at a time when you are not so upset. Tell her you'd like to try again, maybe under different circumstances or with someone else present.

It is not necessary that everything be said at once. You will have made a start. Continuing when emotions are heated will only make things worse. It is okay to try again at another time.

3. *If you are worried that the situation is an emergency, you will need professional guidance as to how to proceed.* Tell the person that you are going to call a professional for advice as to what to do next. Read "No Time to Waste: Emergency Situations" in Chapter 5 for more information as to what to do now.

Anticipating Reactions

You cannot easily predict how someone is going to respond to your overtures. A variety of reactions is possible, and your response will vary depending on what happens. The following sections detail some of the reactions that people commonly have when they are approached about an eating problem.

Relief

For some people, knowing that someone else is aware of the problem affords great relief. They're not alone anymore with their secret, and now there's someone to help them.

Joanne, a 17-year-old bulimic, referred to her discussion with her mother this way:

> After my mother told me that she knew I was bulimic and that she wanted to help me, I felt calm for the first time in a year. I could stop pretending everything was all right with me. I could talk to my parents about some of my feelings. I had been so worried that if my mother found out, she wouldn't be able to take it. Now I didn't have to think about that anymore.

Expressed relief may actually come much later, even years after the confrontation. Marianne, 18, looks back to when she was 15 and her parents insisted she see a psychiatrist for anorexia:

> *I remember screaming at the top of my lungs—no way was I going to some shrink. I was terrified my parents would make me gain weight. I hated them, and I told them so. They didn't know what was best for me.*
>
> *Only now can I admit that I also remember this other feeling underneath saying, "You can stop now. You don't have to fight anymore. You're going to be able to eat." Everything felt quiet inside for the first time in a long time, like a life preserver had been thrown out to me. I remember I just started to cry.*

Admission of a Problem

Sometimes once someone realizes other people are aware of the problem, the person herself is able to admit something is really wrong.

Shelly, a 19-year-old college junior, binged and vomited every night after classes. Because she and her roommate, Derrie, lived in such close quarters, she was sure Derrie knew. Even though Shelly never ate or threw up in front of her roommate, Shelly knew Derrie saw the food and smelled the bathroom odors.

> *Derrie was pretty thin herself, so I just figured she thought the bulimia was not such a bad thing—like I had a good trick to lose weight. But one night Derrie told me that she knew I was bulimic and that she was really upset about it. She said she thought I needed help. I was shocked. I had thought all along that she didn't think it was so bad. When she said this to me, I was embarrassed and for the first time really worried. It was like I finally had to look at what I was doing. Up until then I thought maybe it wasn't so bad if Derrie didn't think so. It was only after that night that I realized I was in trouble and should go for help.*

Some of you may have the fortunate experience of broaching the subject and finding that the person you are worried about is not only aware of the problem but is already in treatment. An important goal has already been achieved, and the road has been paved for an open discussion. (Move on to Chapters 7, 8, and 9.)

Defense and Denial

Not everyone confronted about an eating disorder will react like the teenagers just described. You may find that the person you're approaching denies that a problem exists. Anorexics, in particular, often do not feel they have a problem, and they'll do everything they can to convince you they don't. Bulimics and binge eaters at first may feel nothing but the shame of being found out. Relief is the last thing on their minds at that moment. Remember, you may be the first person talking to them about a secret they may have harbored for years. Your concern may be met with any one of a variety of angry responses.

"How Dare You!"

The person may get furious at you. She may feel intruded upon, embarrassed, found out, and she will react defensively to keep you away. She'll tell you there is no problem—she doesn't know what you are talking about. Be prepared for this possibility; no one likes being confronted with a shame-filled secret. It's important for you to remember that anger is a normal response to the subject you're bringing up. The anger is masking shame and fear, and at this stage, the person may think you are trying to take something away from her.

Be prepared. If you anticipate an angry scene in advance, you'll be better equipped to react to it without getting upset yourself. Don't be intimidated by what the person says. No matter what she is saying, she may very well need you at this point. (Remember Marianne, who could only admit her relief at being found out years later.) Hold your position and repeat why you are concerned. Remember, no matter what the person says, this is not a time for you to react angrily too. It's likely you'll feel angry, but this is not the time to express it.

"Mind Your Own Business"

The person may tell you it's not your business. It's her life, and she can do what she wants. She'll tell you you're always butting in and that if you stopped worrying about her, maybe she wouldn't have a problem in the first place. She'll tell you she can handle things herself. In this case, tell her how her problem is affecting you, how she's made it your business. If you are someone close to her, you might tell her what she has done to make you worry, like losing a frightening amount of weight, isolating herself, or bingeing. Tell her she can't expect someone who cares about her to ignore these behaviors. If you live with her, perhaps she's regularly eaten all the household food or spent long hours in the bathroom when you want to use it. That is certainly your business. Tell her that if she could handle things herself, she wouldn't have given you cause to worry. That's why you feel you have to intervene.

Regardless of exactly what you say, remain firm. Remember too that all of this will be useless if it is said in an angry, accusatory tone. You can be insistent without being upset or demanding.

"You're Not So Great Yourself"

Since the best defense is a good offense, you may find yourself attacked when you bring up this issue. The person may tell you that you're no judge of how someone should eat because you're too fat yourself. Or she might say that *you* diet all the time: what gives you the right to say anything? You count calories too. You worry about your weight. Or she may accuse you of other problems—your drinking, your poor relationships, your own vices and fears. She'll know exactly what to say to make you question yourself.

Don't get pulled into these discussions. It doesn't matter what your problems are at this moment. In fact, you might tell her that if she is worried about something you do, you two can find another time to talk about it. That is not the issue right now. You might start to feel insecure about what you're saying—"How *can* I help? I have my own problems." If you start to say this to yourself, stop! Of course you have problems— we all do—but this doesn't mean you can't be helpful to someone else.

"You're Wrong"

The other person may simply say that you're wrong. She'll tell you that you're just panicking or that you're not living with her, so how could you know, anyway? She'll tell you everyone diets and that she's no different—or that she has a nervous stomach, and the vomiting has nothing to do with bulimia.

You must remember that it is always possible that you *are* wrong. Because you suspect a problem does not always mean that one exists. Tell the other person that you realize this is a possibility. You are prepared to be wrong. However, point out what you *have* seen, why you *are* worried. Tell her at this point that you still have questions and would like to talk about them.

Now What?

When Things Go Well

The other person may be able to acknowledge that she too is concerned about herself. Or she may disagree that a problem exists but seem willing to talk. She may start out resentful but ultimately be able to consider what you have to say. In these cases, you have gotten off to a good start.

With the problem out in the open, it is now important that you follow through with the goals of your discussion. If (such as in the case of friends) you just wanted to let the person know you're concerned, then you have already accomplished what you set out to do. Perhaps you can discuss together how you may continue to be of support. Most likely, though, your goal will involve helping the person evaluate whether a problem exists or what needs to be done next. In fact, if you are concerned about a child or teenager, you will probably need to arrange for the person's treatment yourself. Chapter 6 will guide you in the steps you need to take next. Perhaps you want to speak with the person about how her eating behaviors are interfering in your life, or how you are concerned in general about your relationship with her. Chapters 7, 8, and 9 will provide guidelines for this.

Karen, a 16-year-old anorexic, describes her experience of being approached by her parents:

> I was eating less and less, but I felt so fat that no matter what my parents
> said about how thin I was, I still wouldn't eat. I could hear my parents

arguing about what to do. My mother wanted to leave me alone; she thought it was just a phase I was going through. My father was frightened and thought I should be forced to eat. That fight went on for a long time, and meanwhile I wasn't eating. Then one day, and I don't know how it happened, my parents together said they had to speak to me. I said I had nothing to say to them, but they said, "You don't have to say anything. Just listen."

Then they said, "We love you too much to let you do this to yourself. You're wasting away. You don't go out anymore, you don't see your friends, and we're worried. We spoke to a therapist who specializes in anorexia, and we made an appointment for all of us to see her." At first I told them I wouldn't go. But neither one of them would budge. They said I had no choice. Usually when they would try to tell me what to do, I would get them off my back by listing all their faults. Sometimes I would just complain about one to the other. I tried all this, but neither one took the bait—so here I am.

Deborah, a 26-year-old bulimic, was first confronted about her behavior by her husband:

I'd been married two years, and I was bulimic the whole time. Before I was married, I'd been bulimic for eight years. For two of those years I was still living with my family. I ate more food at dinner than everyone in the family combined, yet I was the thinnest.

After meals I would spend an hour throwing up in the bathroom. No one ever said anything.

Then I got married and did the same thing, and my husband never said anything either. So I figured if they didn't care about me, why should I? I really thought no one noticed. But one day, my husband said he had to talk to me. He told me how hard it was for him to bring this up. He was afraid I would be angry at him, but he said he couldn't live with himself any longer if he didn't say anything. He said my health was more important than my being angry at him. He knew I was bulimic, and he said he was scared about what that meant for him and for me. We were planning to have children, and he was afraid it might interfere with my getting pregnant. It made him feel badly that I kept things secret from him. He wanted me to get some help—maybe go to therapy or attend a support group—and he said he would come too if that would help. He told me he loved me and would do anything to help me. He was crying when he told me all this, and my husband never cried. Being bulimic makes me feel so ashamed that I never thought anyone would want me if they found out about it. His support made me able to face it myself.

Missed Attempts

Bringing up your concerns will not always go well. A mother called us in tears about a confrontation she'd had with her 17-year-old bulimic daughter, Kathy. She suspected her daughter was bulimic and had tried to speak to her about it.

I knew something was wrong with Kathy. Food was disappearing from the kitchen, and she never ate in front of anyone. I found empty laxative boxes in the wastebasket, and she spent much longer than anyone needs to in the bathroom. This morning I went to the bathroom. It stank from vomit. Something inside me snapped. I went into Kathy's room and screamed, "What's the matter with you? Are you sick? What kind of person does this kind of thing?" She was quiet and didn't say anything. I felt desperate to say something that would have an effect on her. The only thing I could think of to make her stop was this: I told her if she kept doing this, I'd tell all her friends. They thought she was Miss Perfect; wait until *they heard this. She just looked at me like she could see through me and said, "Get out of my room; I hate you, I have nothing to say to you." I left the room, but now I don't know what to do next.*

This mother, out of her frustration, approached her daughter in a way that led to misunderstandings, hurt, and anger. As many of us do in difficult situations, she had let the problem go on without saying anything, hoping it would go away, until she felt overwhelmed. She approached her daughter when she was angry, and, as a result, her daughter defended herself with angry silence and insults.

The mother's goal of stopping the bulimia was an impossible one; defeat was inevitable. It would have been less burdensome had she not walked in with such an overwhelming task on her hands. A more manageable goal would have been just to talk.

She also would have had a much better chance at being understood had she approached her daughter at a calmer moment. She and her daughter had a history of arguing. It may have been unrealistic to think she could have approached such a difficult issue without it ending once again in a fight. In this case, the mother needed support in handling her daughter. One way to achieve this would have been to speak with her husband before she said anything. If she felt she couldn't talk without getting upset, perhaps her husband could have approached their daughter, or they might have done it together. If she were calmer, she might have been able to speak to her daughter in a more collaborative manner. For example: "Kathy, we know you're having problems with food. We're concerned about how much you're eating; we've also heard you throwing up, and that worries us. We want to help you with this, and we want you to know we're here for you. Let's talk about what's going on."

In this case, the husband's presence might have tempered the reaction. If he were not available, and the mother still worried about fighting with Kathy, it may have been helpful for the mother to talk first with a professional before speaking to her daughter. There was no reason that she *had* to do it alone.

In another situation, Marie called us about her husband, George, whom she feared had a problem with food:

> George has always been overweight, but that's not really the problem. I don't mind big men. It's just that in the last few years all he seems to think about is food and his weight. He goes from one diet to another, but nothing seems to work; within a week or two, he's eating whatever he wants again.
>
> The problem is that he never seems happy except for that first day or two he's on a diet. Then he feels hopeful and excited. But as soon as he "blows it," he's back obsessing about what he's eating and how heavy he is. He doesn't want to go out; he just mopes around the apartment— eating! Last weekend, I finally had it. We had been planning to go skiing, and at the last minute (after blowing another diet, of course) he said he was too tired to go. I couldn't believe he was doing this again. I lost it. "You're not too tired," I yelled. "You're too fat—you don't have the energy to do anything except eat." He stopped speaking to me, and I don't know what to do.

Marie, like Kathy's mother, approached her husband when she had lost control of her feelings. She was frustrated and disappointed and certainly was not in a position to be supportive. Because she was approaching George when he had let her down, it was unclear whether Marie's goal was to do anything but retaliate for the disappointment she had experienced. If Marie wanted to fight with George, that was one thing. But if she hoped to change the situation, she would need to speak to George when she had thought through what she needed to say.

A more constructive way to approach George would have been for Marie to say: "George, I love you, but you're so down all the time. You're always shutting me—and everyone else—out. I'm worried about your weight, that something will happen to you physically—but I'm also worried that we're so distant from each other now. I miss you. I want to know how I can help."

What to Do If It Doesn't Work

Bringing a problem out into the open is not always going to go smoothly. You may need to try more than once before you are able to express yourself in a way that can be heard and accepted. If so, let some time pass after your first encounter. Then broach the subject again.

In some cases, no matter what you do or say, there may be a steadfast refusal to talk or to acknowledge your concerns. When that happens, you have to decide what to do next. What you can do is the subject of the following chapter.

5

When She Says Nothing Is Wrong

Coping with Denial

What if the person you care about refuses to consider that a problem exists? Either she denies there is a problem and insists nothing is wrong, or she refuses to take the problem seriously.

Whether you merely suspect a problem or know that one exists, this is inevitably a difficult situation, and you are going to need help. You cannot assess the seriousness of the situation or know what to do next on your own. The assessment of an eating disorder is a complex and difficult task. Even professionals cannot always tell if a problem is part of a temporary phase or is the beginning of a full-blown eating disorder. This is certainly not something that you should expect yourself to know.

You Don't Need to Go It Alone

The best way for you to proceed is to contact a professional for a consultation. The purpose of a consultation in this situation is not necessarily to seek treatment, but to receive help in deciphering the seriousness of what you are observing and, given the complexities of your particular situation, knowing what you can do. Consultations can be anywhere from one to a few sessions.

When you go for a consultation, you should let your daughter, spouse, or friend know that you take the situation seriously enough to speak with someone. You should let her know what you are doing, but it is not necessary for you to have her consent. Seeking help is for *you* to find a way of better coping with or handling a situation that is difficult for you. If treatment is in fact needed, and your intervention results in the person seeking help, therapy will be *much* more effective if the eating disorder has been in existence for a short duration. Therefore, it is critically important that you seek a consultation when you first suspect there is trouble. Even though it may be frightening or difficult to confront your child or spouse, the good that may come in initiating a discussion early on far outweighs any conflict that may occur by bringing it up. *Don't second guess your inclination to get help—don't* put it off or give up. A professional can always tell you if it's better to back off.

There are many types of professionals or groups you can contact to help you know how to proceed. For example, you may want to contact an eating disorder specialist or center, a peer support group, or perhaps a hotline. If you are in a college setting, the available resources would include the college health services and a dorm counselor. In work settings, there may be employee assistance programs where counselors are available. The types of resources available are explained in Chapter 6.

Consult the Resources section at the back of the book for organizations that will help you find therapists and treatment facilities in your community.

Before you actually call or set up an appointment to speak with someone, it is a good idea to organize your thoughts:

- Have a clear idea of the behaviors you see that are worrisome. Look over the checklists in Chapter 1 and make a list of the various signs and symptoms you've seen.
- Think about whether there has been a worrisome change in the person's behavior or mood. Can you tell when these changes began? How long have they been going on?
- If you know of or suspect any drug or alcohol abuse, let the consultant know of this.
- The consultant should be particularly alerted to any alarming behaviors, such as talk of suicide, suicidal gestures, and self-mutilating behaviors (for example, cutting). Does the sufferer complain of physical problems, such as fainting, heart palpitations, or shortness of breath?
- Evaluate if and how the impact of the eating behavior has been disruptive in the household. For example, is food missing? Are bathrooms left messy? Are mealtimes stressful?
- If there has been a change in your relationship, let the consultant know what this change is and how long it has been going on. For example, are you arguing more? Does she spend less time with you?
- Tell the consultant what you have tried to do about the situation and what have been the results. Describe discussions or confrontations you have had with the person about whom you're worried and what her reactions have been.

Plans of Action

Depending on your situation, some plans of action may work better than others. What you are advised to do will take into account how severe the situation appears to be, the person's age, her capacity to care for herself, and your relationship to her. What you are advised to do will also depend on the leverage you have in the relationship, that is, the amount of control and/or influence you can exert in this particular relationship.

There are no clear-cut rules as to how to proceed. Each situation differs, and that is why the opinion of a professional or advice of a support group is necessary at these times. The following are some examples of how different families, spouses, and friends were advised to act in their particular situations.

The Steiner Family

This is what Joel and Alicia Steiner were advised to do with their 15-year-old visibly anorexic daughter, who was severely underweight but refused to acknowledge a problem or to see a therapist:

When Alicia Steiner called us, her daughter, Lee, at five feet, five inches, had already dropped from 110 pounds to 90 pounds. The Steiners had not called sooner because Lee had angrily refused to see anyone for help, and they didn't feel there was anything they could do. But as Lee grew thinner and thinner and became isolated from friends, her mother felt they could no longer sit back.

We asked Alicia how it was that a 90-pound teenager was more powerful than her. Lee was potentially dying, and she was not in a position to know what was best for her. How was it that she was the one making all the decisions? We told Alicia that she had to bring Lee in for a consultation. This was not to be Lee's choice.

Alicia feared a scene. She imagined herself and her husband literally carrying a kicking, screaming teenager into our offices. We realized this was possible, but it was still a better option than letting Lee die. With our urgent support behind the Steiners, an interesting thing happened. Alicia and Joel were able to be forceful (verbally, not physically) with Lee, and Lee came into treatment—sulking, but without the tantrum we had all expected. What was clear was that in other attempts to get Lee in for a consultation, the Steiners had backed down when Lee got angry. When Lee realized her parents meant business, she yielded to their authority.

The Robertson Family

In another situation, a parents' support group encouraged the parents of an anorexic daughter to use financial leverage as a way of bringing their daughter into treatment. There are times when withdrawal of financial support may be helpful as a means of showing that you mean business. A symptomatic daughter who is in a life-threatening situation cannot have the freedom to make her own decisions. The Robertsons are an example of how one family used the withdrawal of money to intervene in a potentially harmful situation.

Jenny and Lou Robertson attended a parents' group because they were desperate about how to handle the situation with their 24-year-old daughter, Carey. Carey was planning to spend the year abroad, pursuing her career in art history by attending classes in Italy. Her acceptance to these classes was a long-awaited opportunity, and the Robertsons had decided to pay Carey's expenses as a belated graduation gift. Carey had spent the previous year eagerly planning and anticipating this move. In the past three months, however, the Robertsons had grown concerned that something was wrong. It seemed as if Carey had stopped eating.

Whenever the family got together, she refused meals, choosing to go to her room and exercise instead. She repeatedly asked her older sisters whether she looked fat. When Carey and her mother went shopping for clothes for the trip, Jenny realized that her once normal-weight daughter had dropped at least two clothing sizes in the last several months. In fact, at one point, they had to go to the children's department to find anything that would fit. Carey was delighted. Her mother was horrified. She could see her daughter was not well—and she was about to leave the country for a year.

The members of the support group insisted that the Robertsons question why they were going to support Carey's trip to Europe when Carey was clearly anorexic and in trouble. The Robertsons protested the group's suggestion. This was a promise they had made to their daughter. She had been planning this for a year. Wouldn't she get worse if they withdrew their support? Wouldn't she hate them for doing this?

The group remained firm. They told the Robertsons that they had to tell Carey that they could not pay for this trip because she was in trouble and needed help. She was not taking care of herself in the States; how would she feel alone in Europe? Carey had to see a professional who could determine whether she was healthy enough to continue plans for the trip. It might be possible that help could be set up for her in Europe. Chances were more likely, however, that Carey would need to postpone the trip until her feet were on the ground.

The Robertsons ended up taking the group's advice, but they dreaded the confrontation with Carey. When they spoke to Carey, they told her that they would be ignoring a serious problem if they supported the trip. They said that their financial support would be contingent upon her going for a consultation and having a professional determine whether she was healthy enough to go. Carey blew up. "You promised me!" she screamed. "I can't believe you're backing out of a promise. I've been looking forward to this for a year, and *now* you say something? If you're so worried, why didn't you say anything sooner?"

With the "voices" of the parents' support group behind them, the Robertsons held firm. "We're sorry we didn't take this action earlier," they said. "We have given this a lot of thought, and we're afraid that if we go along with the trip, we will just be paying attention to the part of you who is competent and successful. But there is another part of you who doesn't have a voice who is scared, and worried, and doesn't know what to do. If we let you go, we will be ignoring a big part of you. We feel horrible about this, but we can't ignore how troubled you seem."

Carey screamed that she wasn't troubled—*they* were troubled, and they were certainly going to make her troubled now. She told her parents that they weren't trustworthy and that they were ruining her life. Carey's remarks stung, but the Robertsons kept telling themselves that the group (and even they themselves) knew this was the right decision. Ultimately, there was nothing Carey could do. Jenny Robertson set up the consultation herself, and both parents accompanied Carey to the meeting. The therapist agreed that Carey was in deep trouble and supported the Robertsons in postponing the financing of the trip.

Despite being upset, Carey started treatment.

Doing what the Robertsons did is not easy. Carey was enraged at their decision, insisting she was okay. However, if the Robertsons had backed down, they would have neglected a part of Carey that could only speak up through the weight loss—the skinny, scared little girl who felt overwhelmed by the prospect of a year in another country. By telling Carey they would not endorse or pay for the trip at this point, they were acknowledging Carey's inability to take adequate care of herself at this time.

Ben and Janet Walker

If you are married to someone with an eating disorder, you cannot make unilateral decisions about your spouse. Taking a firm stand about how the problem is hurting you, your spouse, and your relationship will usually get the person's attention and can be a first step in gaining his or her cooperation.

Ben Walker, 35, describes how he approached his wife, Janet, 33, about her bulimia:

> For months, things seemed to be going wrong in our marriage. Janet complained I worked too much; I thought she was depressing to be around—always complaining about her weight when I thought she looked fine. I know the two of us were spending less and less time together—to be honest, I think I was hiding out in my work. But one weekday I got a call at work from our friend, Liz. Liz said that every time she called Jan, she was told that it was a "bad time." "Is she okay?" Liz wanted to know. "I haven't seen her in weeks, and she and I used to speak every day."
>
> Liz's call jolted me and made me wonder if I was missing something that was going on with Jan. When I started to pay more attention, I noticed that Janet was in the bathroom far too often, and when she wasn't in the bathroom, she'd be eating. It occurred to me that not only was Jan putting Liz off, but she wasn't in touch with anyone anymore.
>
> I told Janet I wanted to speak with her. Janet had once talked about having had a history of bulimia, but she hadn't referred to it in years.

This time, I told her what I'd been observing and about Liz's call. I said that I knew things weren't great between us and that I was worried that I was making her sick. I was trying to be caring and open, but she just looked at me and said, "You're not making me do anything." I wanted to know what she was going through. She said, "Nothing. Why are you suddenly so interested, anyway?" I couldn't believe she was being so cold when I was trying to reach out to her. That morning was a disaster. I started yelling at her, and she cried; we ended in silence.

I guess, though, that it scared me. In the afternoon I found the name of a bulimia hotline and spoke to them about Jan. They suggested that I try again but in a different manner.

This time I stayed firm. I told Jan that our marriage was in trouble. We could either let it die or try to do something about it. I wanted to talk about what we could do. I told her that for the marriage to work, I needed her to speak to someone about her bulimia. But it wasn't all up to her; I wanted to know what she needed from me.

I think that this way of talking surprised Jan. I guess she expected more of an attack. When I told her that I was willing to do something too, she was more willing to talk to me.

We went to see a couples therapist. Once we were in treatment, Jan was able to talk about how her worries about our marriage made her want to block everything out by eating. She acknowledged her eating problem and began to work on it. On my part, I had to deal with my own eagerness to retreat through working. In fact, the therapist kept saying that my working was as much of an addiction as Jan's eating. We both had a lot of work to do to get our marriage back on track.

Laura and Jessica—Roommates

In some cases, particularly when friends and colleagues are involved, you will not be advised to further confront the sufferer. Instead, a professional or counselor (such as a dorm counselor or employee assistance program counselor or teacher) will intervene directly by speaking to the person herself. Laura and Jessica were in such a situation.

Laura and Jessica were roommates at a midwestern university. They didn't know each other before rooming together, but by luck they got along perfectly.

When they first arrived at school and were homesick, they could talk to each other. No matter what happened at school or socially, whether times were exciting or disappointing, they could handle it together. Freshman year was turning out better than either had hoped.

Then, in the second semester, Laura noticed a change in Jessica. Suddenly, Jessica always had an excuse for why she wasn't coming to the dining hall. Before, they would order pizzas when they had a late study night. Now Jessica was never hungry. She didn't want late-night snacks. Laura thought Jessica's behavior was strange, and she asked Jessica why she didn't seem to eat much anymore. Jessica would answer that she did eat, it was just at different times, and because Laura didn't see her didn't mean she wasn't eating.

Laura wanted to believe Jessica. She knew Jessica was losing weight, but Laura didn't think too much about it. One night when Jessica thought Laura was sleeping, Jessica undressed in their room instead of in the bathroom. Laura was horrified. She'd never seen anyone in the flesh who looked so thin. The only people Laura had seen that looked like that were in photographs: they were the pictures of concentration camp survivors. But no one who had access to food could look like that.

Laura didn't know what to do. The dorm counselor had lectured all the residents about anorexia nervosa and its effects. She wanted to help Jessica but knew if she told the counselor, Jessica would never speak to her again. If she didn't tell anyone, Jessica might die. Then again, this could just be a phase, and Jessica would start eating again. Perhaps Laura could figure out some way to help Jessica that wouldn't involve telling any of the school authorities.

Unfortunately, Jessica would hear nothing of Laura's concern. She told Laura to mind her own business. Laura was stunned. Jessica had never spoken to her like this before. "I can't stand to watch you do this to yourself," she told Jessica. "You need help. I'm going to speak to our dorm counselor."

"Speak to whomever you want," Jessica sarcastically responded.

Laura did speak to the counselor, who then insisted on speaking with Jessica. School authorities were alerted, and Jessica's parents were contacted. Laura's actions resulted in Jessica's taking a year's leave from school, going into a treatment facility, and getting help.

"I hated Laura that whole year," says Jessica, now 22 and recovered from anorexia. "But now I think she saved my life."

No Time to Waste: Emergency Situations

Some situations are emergencies, and an immediate treatment evaluation is imperative. The situations we are referring to involve the potential of suicide, physical harm, or death due to starvation.

Suicide attempts are not common but at times can occur as a result of the torment and despair associated with an eating disorder, If someone tries to kill herself, if she makes a gesture (such as toying with a razor blade on her wrist), if she even just *tells* you she wants to kill herself, there is reason to consider the situation an emergency. You need to call for help at once. In these cases, it is better to overreact than do nothing.

In the bulimic population, we sometimes see people who cut their bodies superficially without the intent of killing themselves. Cutters explain that when they hurt themselves, they are not trying to die, but that the physical pain contains and narrows the emotional pain. "When I scratch myself with a nail, suddenly everything gets quiet, and all my focus goes on that one little part of my body. If I'm upset or angry, I feel like I have to do it. And then suddenly everything is calm." While cutting is not necessarily an attempt at suicide, it is nonetheless potentially dangerous. If you know someone is cutting, you must insist that she see someone as soon as possible for a consultation.

In some situations talk of suicide (or cutting) can be a daily occurrence in which you are held hostage. Although each threat may not require an intervention, you should not evaluate this on your own: professional assessment is needed.

The other emergency situation involves the possibility of death due to physiological damage. While death occurs less often among bulimics than anorexics, there have been cases of heart failure in both populations. Anorexics can die of many complications secondary to starvation, in particular fluid and electrolyte imbalances. "Fluid imbalance" means that the person is dehydrated; "electrolyte imbalance" refers to potassium depletion, which can cause heart failure. Unfortunately, these imbalances often occur without ongoing signs of something being wrong. Therefore, it should be considered an emergency if someone faints, collapses, or is too weak to walk. While you may know that someone is severely eating disordered by her low weight or constant vomiting, the signs of physical deterioration we have just described may be the only way of knowing that the person might be courting death. Again, you must act immediately and call for help.

In these cases, the person is likely in serious danger and requires immediate attention. If you are a parent, spouse, or friend, this means that you will be told to take the person to a hospital or a doctor for evaluation at once. Don't expect the other person to be a participant in getting help. Certainly you want to approach her in the manner we have been describing all along. Be calm and firm. Tell the person why you are alarmed, why the situation must be taken seriously, and what you are going to do (that is, that you will take her to a doctor or a hospital for an evaluation). Certainly hear her out; give her time to talk. But it's likely that this will not be a good time for a calm discussion. Anticipate that she may refuse to go; you will probably be met with a fight. But no matter how fierce her battle, she has no choice here. When someone is this physically debilitated or psychologically distressed, she is not in a position to be able to judge what is best for her. You must do *whatever* is needed to make sure she will receive immediate professional help.

If you are an acquaintance or roommate, or if you are not an adult yourself, you may not be in a position to assist the person on your own. If that is the case, other professionals (such as school or dorm counselors) may intervene to take care of the person in trouble. If there are no authorities or professionals available, you may need to contact the family. This is not the time to worry about politeness or confidences; someone may be in real danger.

When You Need to Leave It Be

In contrast to emergency situations, there are times when the best thing to do is to leave the situation alone. Eating disorders receive a lot of attention in the media, and you may find yourself sensitized to and worried about an eating behavior that is not a signal of a serious problem but part of a phase. These are times when you will be advised by a professional that your worries are ill-founded. In this situation, it is best to leave things alone and not pursue the matter with the other person. In these cases, pushing the issue when you've been told to leave it alone might only create a power struggle in which the other person may continue eating (or not eating) as a way of doing what *she* wants to do, not what *you* want. A problem can develop where none would otherwise have existed. If you are not convinced, get a second opinion. If you are once again told not to worry, catch your breath, pull back as best you can, and know you can reevaluate the situation in a couple of months if nothing changes.

Accepting Your Limitations

No matter what action is called for, even in the most extreme circumstances, there will always be limits to how effective you can be in influencing someone else's behavior. You may not be able to ensure that someone seeks or stays in therapy or, even if she does, that anything will change.

Shelley, the mother of Tamara, a 24-year-old, had spent the last 10 years grappling with her daughter's bulimia and anorexia. Tamara had been in multiple hospitals and outpatient programs. The only change that Shelley saw was her daughter's fluctuating from anorexia to bingeing to relentless bulimia. Her daughter was always in therapy (Shelley didn't even want to think how much it had cost), and at this point, she was being encouraged by Tamara's therapist to step back and let Tamara take hold of her own life, no matter what that looked like.

The last time Tamara came home for a visit, her clothes were once again hanging on her, and despite the sultry, 94-degree weather, Tamara kept her jacket on the entire day. Shelley hit the roof.

These kinds of situations are terrifying and maddening. They cause you to face the stark limitations of being a parent, spouse, or friend. No matter what you do, the other person is not going to change her behavior or seek help until she is capable of accepting the seriousness of the matter herself. You are not going to be able to make her see what you see or do what you may know is best.

When you are faced with this kind of helplessness, you absolutely must speak to someone else—not about the person in trouble, but about yourself and what has happened to your life. This is why this book was written—not just because there are things you can do, but often, and sometimes more importantly, because sometimes there are things you can't do. When what you can't do is save your daughter, your wife, your friend, the feelings that ensue are bound to be overwhelming. Here, you can't go it alone.

Chapters 7, 8, and 9 are devoted to discussing the process of recovery—your recovery as well as that of the person you love. There are many steps you can take to help someone turn in the right direction to change her life. But there are also many things you can do about changing the effect the eating disorder has on your life, and allowing for recovery of your own well-being in the relationship you have with the sufferer.

6

No One Can
Go It Alone

Seeking Help

It has now been well over 20 years since eating disorders first emerged as a significant problem among young women in our culture. Treatments have developed, evolved, and changed as a result of learning more about what is needed both psychologically and physiologically. Initially, we were excited and hopeful that we could develop a treatment protocol that would stop these disorders in their tracks. However, while we have made significant progress in allowing for change, many directions have emerged as potential answers, not just one. The question these days is not whether there is help for someone who is eating disordered. The question more often is what direction to take and at what juncture—and most pertinently now, how families can best be of help.

Treatment Planning for the Eating-Disordered Person

When someone who is eating disordered is in need of services, she should be seen for a consultation with a professional who can help outline the type of treatment approach that would be most beneficial. Even at this first juncture, questions arise. Should the initial evaluation be done by a physician who can assess physical damage or by a psychologist or social worker who can consider the psychological aspects of the problem at hand? What medication can be used? Should an evaluation be done by a nutritionist?

Often a physician skilled in eating disorders is the first professional to consult. A physician should be able to determine whether eating behaviors have resulted in compromised health. For example, heart rate may be low, potassium levels may be unbalanced, and weight may be dropping quickly. Only a physician familiar with eating disorders can assess whether a person is in need of treatment, and if so, whether that means immediate hospitalization or less urgent intervention on an outpatient basis. A knowledgeable physician can assess how someone is eating and can evaluate whether there are signs of a problem developing (such as missed breakfasts, avoidance of fats, and binge eating). The doctor also may be able to allay fears, telling worried parents that, for example, while their daughter is thin, she is not at all unhealthy and does not show signs of anorexia.

If a physician assesses that a problem does indeed exist, but that more urgent inpatient care is not needed, the next consultation that is needed is with a therapist trained in the treatment of eating disorders. There, a treatment plan will be set up, spelling out what kinds of treatment are needed and how the family can best be involved. The treatment plan takes into account many factors, including the onset, duration, and severity of the illness, the family situation, and other substance abuse. The consultant will consider the situation and will then recommend a course of treatment that may include work with different specialists or groups.

If a physician doesn't think a problem exists and you still are worried, it is important to get a second opinion. A psychologist or social worker (again, skilled in eating disorders) can help you understand what may be wrong and what needs to change—even if it isn't clear that an eating disorder exists.

There are times when the person you care about may want to see a nutritionist as the first course of action. A nutritionist can outline a supportive and structured direction to take regarding food intake and healthy eating. While a consultation with a physician is always recommended, sometimes the focused work of a nutritionist is all that is needed to get someone back on track. If, however, the person is not able to put the nutritional suggestions to use, then a more psychological approach is warranted to understand what is getting in the way.

Psychotherapy

Usually, the most effective means of treating the eating-disordered patient is through the process of psychotherapy. Different types of psychotherapy are possible, such as individual, family (including couples treatment), and group therapy. The type of therapy recommended will depend on the age, needs, and living situation of the person seeking treatment. Often, the person with the disordered eating will need her own individual treatment in addition to anything else recommended so that she can have a place to recognize her own needs and develop her own voice, separate from her family or spouse.

One factor that is evaluated in treatment planning is whether the person has any other problems in addition to the eating disorder. Is she, for example, a multiple abuser who also has trouble with drugs and/or alcohol? Most professionals agree that alcohol and drug abuse needs to be controlled before active work on the eating disorder is undertaken. Thus treatment planning will need to take this into account.

An assessment should also be made of other factors in the life and family of the eating-disordered person. Is there gambling, incest, alcohol and/or drug abuse, or violence at home? Sometimes treating someone with an eating disorder will involve addressing these issues in family or couples therapy. Therefore, a treatment plan needs to consider all these possibilities.

Individual Psychotherapy

In individual psychotherapy, the patient meets with the therapist alone. Sessions are held a minimum of once a week, usually lasting 45 minutes per session.

Individual psychotherapy of the eating-disordered person should involve working with the visible symptoms of bingeing, purging, or starving and the more "invisible" psychological factors.

The eating behavior itself needs to be discussed. Indeed, this is what is foremost on the person's mind. The person in therapy works to understand the role that eating or purging has served in her life and finds replacements for the destructive behaviors while developing healthier coping mechanisms.

As she explores her inner world and her experiences with people, she comes to understand why and how eating (or starving) has become her means of coping. Why is it that food is safer than turning to people?

Why does nothing else feel as soothing as the eating or purging? What keeps getting in the way of her resolve to stop bingeing? What would be on her mind if she weren't worried about her weight?

Not every type of individual psychotherapy will address underlying feelings and thoughts. The treatment we endorse is one that will focus on changing the eating behaviors without losing sight of the reasons why food is used in the first place. The goal of treatment should not be merely to stop the behavior, but to understand *how* and *why* the person has used food to attempt to meet developmental and emotional needs. Don't assume because someone is a therapist that he or she will necessarily work in this fashion.

There are two pitfalls that should be avoided. The first is where the symptom is focused on to the exclusion of its purpose in the person's life. If treatment addresses the visible aspects of the problem and does not consider what is unseen—the psychological factors—the problem is apt to continue via other means. Many women switch from food to alcohol or drugs in their attempts to control their eating. Without understanding the way the food helps them, they merely replace one addiction with another.

The other pitfall involves a treatment focus that is concerned solely with the inner world of the patient. We hear too often of therapy that has been going on for many years and food is not discussed at all. This is like treating an active alcoholic without addressing the alcohol abuse. When someone is actively bingeing or starving and it is not being discussed in detail, with direct interventions aimed at changing the behaviors, only half the person is in the treatment room.

One of the main benefits of individual therapy is that it provides a one-to-one relationship with the therapist, in which the person in treatment can acknowledge and explore her feelings and thoughts. As the eating-disordered person is more fully able to accept herself as well as her feelings about others, the need to block out parts of herself through food can be lessened. One aspect of this is helping her differentiate feelings from physiological hunger. People with eating disorders tend to misinterpret internal emotional experiences as hunger and respond by eating.

The therapist should be a person who is not involved in the patient's personal life. He or she should not be a relative or friend of the family. This way, the patient can feel assured that the therapist has no personal investment in what she does, and she can feel safer to reveal feelings and thoughts about herself, family, and/or friends.

Family Therapy

In recent years, the role of the family in the treatment of eating disorders has taken center stage. In particular, with the treatment of adolescent anorexics and sometimes bulimics, the question looms as to how involved the parents and family should be in the actual feeding of their child. A treatment plan called the Maudsley approach (named after the London hospital where British researchers developed this program) urgently advocates parental involvement in the refeeding and care of one's eating-disordered child or teenager. With the guidance of a family therapist, parents are taught, for example, how to slowly and gently insist that their anorexic child eat, very much like the nursing staff does with inpatient anorexics. This control continues until one's daughter is at a body weight within normal limits, or until she has stopped bingeing and purging and is eating healthy meals. Then the therapist helps the parents to gradually give up control of the eating and at the same time to treat their daughter in more age-appropriate ways in other areas of her life.[14]

If you have a child or teen who is clearly eating disordered, it is very likely that you have already tried to change her eating and distorted thoughts about her body and food intake. You have probably reasoned with her, thought of award systems and bribes. You've tried to be encouraging. You've certainly lost your temper. All of this is normal. If these interactions with your daughter are working and the eating is significantly changing, you may be on the right track. Just make sure to pay attention and remember that these problems are not just about food. If the hidden parts of the disorder are not addressed, it is likely that problems will soon reemerge.

More than likely, however, your efforts to help refeed your daughter or control her bingeing episodes have not gone smoothly. This is why we have written this book. Controlling your daughter's food intake may not always be the best solution. The decision as to whether or not you should be involved in feeding your child is usually one that should not be made alone. A well-trained family therapist comfortable with this approach can assess whether feeding interventions will help or not. Merely just trying to get your daughter to eat is not the Maudsley approach and most likely will end up in a control battle, and the situation will worsen. When feeding is undertaken within the context of family therapy, the goal is not only to have your daughter gain weight, but to restructure the family system. The goal is to put you as parents back in charge, united in your position with your daughter regarding her eating. Although the process begins with your taking control, in the long run it helps you to separate from your child, paving the way for her to grow up. Only when the feeding is undertaken in this larger context can it be helpful in treating the young anorexic.

Tamara and Jack Colby had watched helplessly as their 14-year-old daughter Kristen's weight plummeted from a healthy 118 pounds (at five feet, five inches) to a skeletal weight of 87 pounds. No matter what they did, the weight continued to drop. They had taken Kristen to meet with both a therapist and an internist when they realized her weight had initially dropped, but nothing anyone did seemed to help. The next year Kristen spent in and out of hospitals.

Finally, Tamara and Jack decided to take things into their own hands. They had been reading about the Maudsley approach and decided to seek out a therapist who would help the family work in this way. They decided to dedicate as much time as was needed to getting Kristen steady again. This was no minor task. Kristen was home from school and hospitals at this point. Tamara put her job on hold, and Jack minimized any outside involvements he had previously had, separate from his job. Their 16-year-old son would be away at camp, so they had the summer to dedicate to the task of getting Kristen well.

Every day, Tamara sat with Kristen for at least two hours each meal. The calories of every bite of food were assessed, and while Kristen could choose what type of foods she would eat, Tamara and Jack insisted on the amounts. Kristen was sullen, angry, and determined not to gain weight. But Tamara and Jack were equally as determined and wouldn't budge. Tamara did most of the actual work, sitting with Kristen, cajoling, pushing, and making it clear that Kristen couldn't do anything else but finish her meal. Sometimes they would watch TV while eating, or they would listen to music—there could be distractions, but Kristen had to eat. Jack supported Tamara, and when Tamara was just too frustrated, he took over with the feeding. Slowly, Kristen got into a routine regarding the eating. She still needed to know the calories of anything she put in her mouth, and meals were still at least two-hour ordeals, but by the end of the summer, Kristen had gained 10 pounds and was healthy enough to go back to school instead of going back to a hospital.

It is not clear which families benefit from the Maudsley approach and which do not. As a general rule, families in which there is a significant degree of overt hostility or criticism usually do not do well with this method.[15] But each family differs—even families who function well together and who have the best of intentions can be thwarted.

Jay and Debbie Simon came to us for help with their 15-year-old anorexic daughter, Lisa, after having spent several weeks trying to get Lisa to nudge her weight above 92 pounds. She was five feet, four inches, and no one, including Lisa, wanted to see her leave school and be hospitalized. They were working with a doctor, a nutritionist, and a family therapist to help get Lisa back on her feet.

"It's just been hell," Jay reported during a family consultation that was set up to consider what else could be done.

Debbie and I have been doing all the right things—we were patient, we'd sit with Lisa, we told her she had to eat, and we'd be at her side. But she'd sit there and have the worst look on her face, scramble her food around on her plate, and just not eat. My wife, Debbie, sometimes would sit with Lisa for three hours, and still nothing would happen.

I kept holding in my frustration and anger and would stay steady and calm—or just leave the room for a break. I don't know how Debbie could just sit there. But one Saturday we were trying to get out of the house to actually do something fun, and the whole thing was getting delayed, maybe even canceled—and I finally just lost it. I started screaming that Lisa was ruining our family and that she might as well be in a hospital so that things could get back to normal. Debbie started to cry and scream herself, saying that I was ruining the program. Lisa just ran out of the room.

We're just not sure this is something we can do. We don't know how other families do it.

Jay and Debbie were very smart, sophisticated, well-intentioned parents. It was unclear why their work with Lisa was having no effect. They were thoughtful, working closely with a therapist, and questioning themselves at every turn. They wondered if it was something they were doing that they weren't aware of. Jay wondered if Debbie was too involved with the whole eating process. Debbie thought Jay was too involved with his work and not home as much as he thought he was. But in truth, it's unclear what happened in this family. Every family has ways of interacting that aren't perfect. We just don't know enough yet to be able to say what makes one situation successful and another so difficult. Lisa did end up being hospitalized and spent the next year struggling to make changes in her life and her weight. Jay, Debbie, and Lisa used the family therapy to focus on what was needed now, even with hospitalization in the picture, to help Lisa and her parents move on with their own lives both as a family and as individuals, even while the eating disorder was still very much in the picture.

Indeed, for some families, a more traditional approach to family therapy is warranted in which family dynamics are considered, but the feeding is left in the hands of the therapists and professionals.

No matter which direction is taken, family members need to know what to expect with the eating disorder, what is normal, and what their role should be if refeeding is not an option.. Family meetings can allow parents to understand how they can best be of help. Family therapy can also help the family set rules and establish different interactions between parents and children. Communication skills will be improved, which will allow for safer and more effective expressions of feelings and conflict. The goal is not merely to change the eating disorder but to solve the family's problems in a way that all members are encouraged to change.

The course of therapy, the frequency of meetings, and the participants in the sessions will vary depending on the severity of the disorder and the specific family situation. In all of these cases, the goal is still the same. Members work to explore and understand patterns of interacting that interfere with each individual's growth and the family functioning. Sometimes this will mean that the parents are more involved with decisions about their daughter's eating. Other times the best way for the daughter to grow and be responsible for food issues will be for the parents to pull back from the decisions around food. Whether parents are actively involved or not, the goal must be how to help the person take responsibility for her own health and eating. What this means in each family will differ depending on the ages, the duration of illness, and the specific interactions that need to change among family members.

Whether the parents actively intervene or not will likely depend on the developmental strengths of their daughter, her emotional resiliency, and her psychological resources. If the daughter is unable to soothe herself, if she hasn't yet developed coping skills necessary to handle emotionally charged experiences, if her relationships with others are fragile or minimal, it may be that parents need to be a stronger part of the picture. Here their role is not only to directly help with the problematic eating behaviors but also to provide needed ongoing parenting in other arenas. Regardless of the specific situation, the advice of a skilled therapist is invaluable in determining how best to proceed.

Group Therapy

A group usually consists of 5 to 12 people who meet with a therapist on a weekly basis. This treatment approach is particularly helpful in countering feelings of isolation or of being all alone with the problem and is usually used in conjunction with individual psychotherapy. A group can provide feedback and support while someone is attempting to change eating patterns. It is also a safe place for members to learn new ways of relating, to express feelings, and to develop trusting relationships that can substitute for the self-destructive relationship to food.

There are different types of groups. Some focus specifically on the eating and its meaning and function in someone's life. In these groups, the members may concentrate on how and when the eating behavior occurs. Group members support one another in finding ways to change the eating patterns and develop healthier coping styles. Sometimes group members may call one another for support when they are having a rough time with the urge to binge. These types of groups are usually time-limited, organized to last anywhere from several weeks to several months.

Other groups are more insight-oriented and do not focus exclusively on the eating behaviors, but address underlying emotional dilemmas as well. They are usually open-ended in duration.

The difference between the two types of groups is highlighted by Terry's experience. Terry, 25, had been attending a behavior-oriented group in addition to her individual therapy. The group focused on learning what triggered the members' urges to binge and how to develop alternatives to the bingeing behavior. Terry was now looking to move on:

> As a result of this group and my individual therapy, I am able to control my bingeing most of the time, and because of this I rarely vomit. But now I need to take the next step. I want a group that is less focused on food and more on interaction. I know I've used food to avoid people. I need to see what scares me so much about relying on people.

Terry was referred to an insight-oriented group in which she was able to explore her relationships with group members as a way of understanding why she believed that food was more dependable than people.

Outpatient groups are not usually recommended for the treatment of acute anorexia nervosa. Anorexics who are severely restricting their food intake are not able to relate well enough to others to benefit from the interaction. Their cognitive and social capacities are so impaired from starvation that it is impossible for them to concentrate on relationships with other people. In addition, these young women are so intensely competitive about being the thinnest in the room that the usual good feelings that arise from the experience of shared problems and mutual support do not develop. Because of this, the development of trust and mutual respect does not occur. In the structured setting of a hospital or intensive treatment program, however, where weight gain is an inevitable part of the program, groups provide a significant source of support and therapeutic work.

Support or Self-Help Groups

Whether or not someone is in psychotherapy, support or self-help groups can be a valuable means of getting help with the problem and feeling less isolated. These groups consist of people at various stages of recovery who meet to share experiences, suggestions, and camaraderie. For many people, self-help groups are a first step in realizing they are not alone and that change is possible.

Support and self-help groups can meet anywhere from daily to once a month. As the name implies, they are not psychotherapy groups and thus are not necessarily run by a therapist. A leader is present to structure the group meeting. Sometimes the leader is herself recovered from an eating disorder and can use her own experience as a source of inspi-

131

ration and/or guidance for others. Because these groups do not employ the services of a trained professional, they are usually free or are run for a nominal fee to pay for the meeting space that is used. The groups can be attended as needed without participants having to make a commitment to join. As a result, membership can change from meeting to meeting.

Support groups vary in their structure. Some have no particular agenda, while in others, a particular topic is discussed at each meeting. Some groups start with a speaker, then break into small discussion groups, where participants explore their feelings about the subject discussed. Examples of topics that groups have picked to discuss include "How eating disorders affect relationships," "What you should you do if you're hungry," and "How to handle going home for Thanksgiving."

The National Association of Anorexia Nervosa and Associated Disorders (ANAD) has affiliated support groups available both in the United States and internationally. ANAD has developed an eight-step program that encourages shared feelings and personal growth through interaction and support. Other organizations that help develop support groups are listed in the Resources section at the back of the book.

Overeaters Anonymous

Overeaters Anonymous (OA) is a particular kind of self-help group based on the 12-step program for recovery developed by Alcoholics Anonymous. Overeaters Anonymous is based on the philosophy that binge eaters are powerless over food and that eating disorders are life-long addictions. Control over food is sought by helping one another resist the temptations of bingeing. OA now has meetings specifically for bulimics and anorexics.

OA has an extensive support network available for the person who may be craving food at all hours of the day. Members are encouraged to find a sponsor whom they can call when they need help abstaining from bingeing or purging. The sponsor is someone who is at a later stage of recovery and is available to people first entering the program.

Within the philosophy of OA, abstinence is seen as the basis of recovery. However, for many eating-disordered people, abstinence is simply the opposite of bingeing. They may be on the winning side of the battle, but the war wages on. OA does not see the possibility of truly making peace with food. Yet while we believe, as do many others in the professional community, that eating disorders can be curable, not merely controllable, there is a portion of the eating-disordered population that faces a chronic, lifelong struggle with food. For this group, OA offers an invaluable community that provides help in maintaining abstinence from bingeing. For others, the OA program can be turned to at different times during the process of recovery when support and structure are felt to be needed.

Medical and Nutritional Treatment

The varied physiological complications that result from disturbed eating behaviors require the attention of specialists, including internists, dentists, gynecologists, and nutritionists. During a treatment evaluation, the consultant may recommend that one or more of these professionals be seen to evaluate physiological damage or to provide specialized care in their area.

Internists

One cannot assume that an eating disorder is being comprehensively treated unless an internist is involved to assess the potential damages secondary to the eating disturbance. Unattended physical complications in all three disorders can lead to serious health problems and, in the worst case, death. In particular, the treatment of an anorexic must always involve the ongoing active presence of an internist who will monitor health and weight and who will be the one determining whether a higher level of care, such as hospitalization, is needed.

There are many destructive physical complications that can arise from problematic eating or purging patterns. For example, in anorexia nervosa common complications are lowered blood pressure, lowered body temperature, kidney and cardiac disorders, slow pulse rate, bloating, dry skin, and loss of menstrual cycle. When someone suffers from obesity due to binge eating, heart, lung, and circulatory problems need to be evaluated. The symptoms of bulimia are varied. Some are troublesome, such as the loss of menstrual periods, decreased energy, light-headedness, and altered bowel habits. Others, such as irregular heartbeat, abdominal pain, and muscle cramps, may indicate serious complications. Dehydration and loss of important minerals are often the cause of these more serious disturbances.

When laxatives are used, which they might be in any of the three types of eating disorders, other complications can arise. Muscle and stomach cramps, chronic nausea, digestive problems, and physiological dependence are all possible effects of chronic laxative abuse. Patients describe trying to quit laxatives on their own, but if they have grown physiologically dependent upon them, they find that without the laxative intake, their body doesn't function properly. They can't go to the bathroom, and their body blows up like a balloon from water retention. A physician may be needed to prescribe increasingly lower doses of milder laxatives until the body has learned to take over its natural functioning once again.

If someone is seeing a therapist who specializes in eating disorders, the therapist will probably be able to recommend a physician. If not, you or the person in therapy may have to do some hunting around. It is important that professionals are chosen who are familiar with eating disorders and who take them seriously. If your child has shown a recent alarming weight drop and the physician says it is just a phase, look for another physician. If your wife is vomiting to control weight and the doctor merely prescribes diet pills to ease her struggle, you must press her to find another doctor.

Despite the prevalence of bulimia and anorexia nervosa in recent years, many physicians still remain ignorant of the severity and deteriorating course of these problems. The rule of thumb is that if a physician you've contacted does not have a recognition of and respect for the psychological components of these disorders, he or she is not yet sufficiently informed. Move on and find another. The national organizations listed in the Resources section can help guide you in locating informed medical services in your location.

Because the signs and symptoms of an eating disorder are sometimes hidden, it is important that the person see someone who knows the current medical literature on these disorders and who will know to look for the ways the symptoms manifest themselves. The person seeking help should also be encouraged to be open and frank with her physician about her eating behaviors. One bulimic woman went to an internist because she was concerned about the enlarged glands in her throat. She was examined and tested for Hodgkin's disease before she was able to muster the courage to admit that she was bulimic. Chronic swollen glands are a common side effect of bulimia. The internist was unfamiliar with this, and the woman, so embarrassed about the bulimia, was willing to be treated for cancer before she could consider revealing her problem.

If both the physician and patient are open about issues such as bingeing, vomiting, laxative abuse, and starvation, the whole examination procedure will be much more productive.

Dentists

Someone who is vomiting frequently is susceptible to tooth decay as a result of enamel erosion from regurgitated stomach acids. Dentists can be the first to notice these signs of bulimia. A checkup by a dentist is important for anyone who is vomiting.

A well-informed dentist and an open discussion about the problem will facilitate the treatment. Dentists who are unaware that the tooth erosion is due to vomiting may repair the damage without suspecting that the problem is ongoing, and damage to the teeth will continue. As one patient told us in a group:

> I was on my third set of caps and $10,000 poorer, and my dentist couldn't figure it out. Finally, after working on it in therapy, I got up the nerve to tell him what I was doing. He suggested a temporary solution of brushing my teeth with baking soda after I threw up. He told me that the base in baking soda helped counteract the acids from vomiting and that this would slow down the erosion until I was able to stop purging. He also knew to stop replacing my caps.

Gynecologists

Complications due to anorexia nervosa and bulimia may also warrant the services of a gynecologist.

For example, endocrinological changes caused by weight fluctuations and poor nutrition can alter the menstrual and reproductive cycle. Irregular menstrual cycles or a cessation of menses can occur. Studies indicate that weight loss can result in the shrinking of the uterus and ovaries to prepubertal or pubertal size.[16] While this type of physiological regression can be corrected with weight gain, the need for a gynecologist's input to monitor such irregularities is indicated.

Bulimics or anorexics who are vomiting may want to know whether birth control pills will be effective if they are vomiting or taking high doses of laxatives. (In fact, a gynecologist prescribing birth control pills *must* be told of purging behaviors so that the effectiveness of this type of contraception can be assessed.)

If pregnancy is desired, the effects of vomiting, starving, and using laxatives must be taken into account. As indicated above, someone whose menstrual cycle is irregular or whose reproductive organs have been affected by starvation may have trouble getting pregnant.

However, many bulimics and some anorexics who have yet to stop menstruating completely do achieve conception. When conception is possible, the question then is, will the fetus be healthy? There is much to be learned about the effects and risks of chronic vomiting, starving, and laxative abuse on fetal development and the health of the baby. Eating disorders sometimes result in malnutrition, and evidence indicates that severe malnutrition during pregnancy can cause a permanent reduction in fetal brain growth and development, with possible reduction in the baby's intellectual functioning. Even if someone is not eating disordered at the time of pregnancy, studies indicate that a history of bulimia and anorexia may result in a slightly lower live birth rate than what is normally expected and a higher rate of spontaneous abortions.[17]

If the person you know is pregnant or thinking about becoming pregnant, speak with her about this. Her gynecologist must be made aware of her disturbed eating patterns. Urge the person you know to speak with her doctor. She will probably be considered at high risk and can be monitored for the various endocrinological changes caused by the eating disorder.

Some women with eating disorders revert to more normal eating habits during their pregnancy. Gerry, 32, a daily binge vomiter, told us: "When I was pregnant and, in a sense, taking care of someone else, I was able to eat normally, and I kept the food down. But after the baby was born, I went back to my old ways."

A gynecologist aware of current research in the area of eating disorders should be able to answer questions regarding conception, pregnancy, and fetal risk that concern the eating-disordered woman and her partner.

Nutritional Counseling

Nutritionists, who are trained to assess imbalances in food intake and develop dietary programs, can help correct nutritional deficits and guide someone with an eating disorder to develop healthy eating habits, perhaps for the first time. Some people with eating disorders have extremely chaotic eating patterns or have not eaten a "meal" in years.

With anorexics, in particular, nutritional counseling is often a critical part of the therapy. Anorexics are terrified that anything they eat will result in rapid weight gain. A good nutritionist will be able to set up a plan not only in which weight can be gained, but in which weight is gained slowly so that the anorexic feels less out of control and is better able to cooperate with the treatment goals. When weight is gained, brain chemistry and body chemistry start to be repaired. This sets the stage for the patient to be better able to respond to other areas of treatment, such as beginning to identify the connection between thoughts, feelings, and food.

For bulimics and/or binge eaters, the work of a nutritionist is used to establish healthy eating patterns. For example, sometimes food deprivation during the day can lead to bingeing during the night. Nutritional guidance can be invaluable in helping to stabilize food intake and determining what can be eaten without the risk of gaining or losing weight.

Sometimes a nutritionist is sought to provide a diet as an answer to the problems with bingeing. However, a diet is not the answer to an eating disorder. Many eating-disordered people are experts themselves on diets and food intake. They know what is healthy. They know the caloric intake of every morsel they put in their mouths. Some are professionals in the area of nutrition. This underscores that eating disturbances are not due to lack of information about a good diet, but have to do with psychological factors that keep people from putting this information to use. Often, a nutritionist and therapist work concurrently. The nutritionist sets the stage for healthy eating, and the therapist examines what gets in the way when someone can't keep to her food plan. The goal overall is that of allowing someone to eat when hungry, in moderation, and to understand what motivates problematic eating so that better choices can be made.

Medication

Psychopharmacological intervention is now considered to be an important aspect of treatment for a significant portion of eating-disordered patients. The role of physiology with regard to self-soothing, cravings, and addictive behavior is well documented. For example, a depletion of the brain neurochemical serotonin can lead to excessive food cravings. That is why medications like Prozac and Zoloft, which enhance the potential for serotonin in the brain, can be effective in reducing binge behavior.[18] If someone is not able to make any overt changes in the first weeks of treatment, an evaluation for psychopharmacological intervention should be considered. In this case, you will need to meet with a psychiatrist or psychopharmacologist who is well informed with the current research in eating disorders.

For some portion of the eating-disordered population, depression is complicating the situation. For these patients, disturbed eating behaviors develop in an attempt to subdue a biologically based depression. When there are signs of depression, such as lethargy, loss of interest in life, and suicidal thoughts, antidepressant medication must be considered as part of the treatment recommendations. In these cases, treatment of the depression can alleviate the need to binge, purge, or starve.

For other patients, psychopharmacological intervention is used to specifically address the physiologically based cravings and urgency associated with bingeing or vomiting. It is important to note that medications do not suddenly stop an eating disorder. They only help to even out moods and cravings so that the person with the disordered eating begins to feel what other people feel in terms of moods or cravings. From there, the person on medication still has to fight hard to conquer her particular battle with food. The goal of medication is to help someone stay in the battle instead of feeling too overwhelmed to fight.

The most usual concern regarding medication is that having to do with side effects. One of the benefits of the more recently developed groups of medication is that they have significantly fewer side effects than drugs had in years past. However, all medications may still carry some side effects. Prozac, for example, is used to treat depression as well as binge behavior. However, Prozac can sometimes cause low-grade headaches, rashes, or difficulties in sexual functioning, which may need to be addressed with other medication. All drugs must be assessed for potential side effects and should be administered only as part of a well thought out treatment plan, combining therapy and other health-oriented programs. In this context, medication can be important in helping the person delay impulsive eating behaviors and learn to make better choices.

It is crucial to remember that medication is never enough by itself. Don't expect it to passively cure an eating disorder, or you and the sufferer will be sorely disappointed. There are no easy cures or simple answers. The research is evolving, and there are ongoing changes regarding the most effective psychopharmacological intervention. It is of the essence to work with a psychiatrist who actively keeps informed as to the evolution of this field.

Research emphasizes that long-term positive results from medication occur only when medication is part of an integrated treatment plan, including psychotherapy. Medication is not a substitute for developing internal capacities to cope with life and its stressors. Drugs can help abate the urgency to binge or overeat. However, time and again, patients continue to turn destructively to food or purging, despite being on medication that they insist is actually working. Unless the reasons underlying disturbed eating are understood and addressed, the eating-disordered person—medicated or not—will remain vulnerable to maintaining disordered food rituals when faced with difficult times or distressing internal experiences.

Surgery

Recently, bariatric surgery has taken center stage as a treatment modality for the significantly overweight patient. Indeed, in 1991, the National Institutes of Health recommended bariatric surgery for the morbidly obese patient (BMI over 50) or for the morbidly obese patient who has a high risk of comorbid conditions (more than 100 pounds overweight or a BMI of over 40).[19] While only 16,000 patients had gastric bypass or vertical banded gastroplasty in 1992, by 2005, 170,000 patients had had surgery,[20] with the number of patients continuing to grow. The most common type of surgery is the lap-band surgery, a minimally invasive surgery, in which a band is placed around the stomach. Band placement allows the obese person to feel full after eating only a small portion of food, thus allowing weight loss to occur quickly.

It is important to note that while surgery is considered the most effective treatment for the morbidly obese patient, studies are just evolving considering the long-term effect of this kind of treatment and whether this treatment is ultimately helpful for the binge-eating patient. In general, at one and a half to two years postsurgery, weight loss stabilizes, and a substantial portion of individuals even begin to regain lost weight.[21] What is clear is that a presurgical history of binge-eating disorder is associated with poorer long-term weight outcomes. There are many stories of patients who have reached their ideal weight following surgery, only to quickly regain all of the weight once their goal has been reached. In these cases, bingeing begins again despite severe physical pain, vomiting, and the obvious despair of watching the scale skyrocket again. One patient described losing and gaining over 100 pounds in less than two years.

Bariatric surgery thus can initially achieve substantial weight loss, but surgery alone may not alter the underlying eating disorder. If the eating disorder remains, positive results can be significantly compromised. Without a deeper understanding of the psychological role of bingeing, without the possibility of medication to address physiological cravings, and without an ongoing program to develop new means of dealing with feelings and stress, surgery may just be a bandage that only temporarily covers a longer-term and deeper problem.

Hospitalization and Residential Care

When someone is in a psychologically self-destructive or a physically life-endangering condition, hospitalization or other residential care may be necessary (see "No Time to Waste: Emergency Situations" in Chapter 5). If there is the potential for suicide, or daily functioning is severely impaired, then intensive interventions are needed. Impairment in functioning may mean that the person cannot concentrate for sustained periods, her emotions feel overwhelming, and/or the bingeing, purging, or starving behaviors are extreme. When someone is in this condition, outpatient treatment is not effective. The person needs more support and structure than is possible a few hours a week in therapy or support groups. In these cases, reducing the environmental stressors while providing structure and psychotherapy can be useful.

While hospitalization or residential care are essential in severe conditions, it is not always necessary to wait for such a crisis before it can be helpful. It need not be a last resort. When used thoughtfully and effectively, there are times when these programs can provide a safe environment in which the patient can regain the inner resources and experience the sense of control needed to cope in her daily life. Here there is an opportunity to interrupt the symptomatic eating patterns and allow the person to explore areas of concern that could not be approached if the eating were out of control.

With anorexia, in particular, the possibility of hospitalization is often used to motivate the person to gain weight. Over the years, professionals have found that with anorexics, just talking about one's feelings and experiences often does not lead to change in the starving behavior. A better approach is usually to set a weekly goal weight that the patient is expected to achieve, with the plan that hospitalization will occur if the goal is not met. In these cases, the family may or may not be engaged in the refeeding, and there should be ongoing exploration of the psychological and familial factors involved in the maintenance of the symptom. But often the most motivating force for the anorexic to gain weight is the fear that she will land in a hospital if she doesn't meet particular goal weights. This should not be presented merely as a threat but more as a matter of fact. That is, if someone can't make use of outpatient treatment, she is unwittingly calling out for a higher level of care.

When hospitalization is considered, the initial evaluation process must assess the potential benefit of inpatient care in abating symptomatology and compare that with the disruption that an inpatient stay might cause. If residential care or hospitalization is recommended for extended treatment, it is critically important that the program has a specialty in eating disorders. No matter how excellent a facility's reputation, if meals are not monitored and weight assessed, the disordered eating may well continue despite the best therapeutic efforts. A general psychiatric unit is usually not the answer. A medical unit that attends solely to weight is also inadequate. There are now facilities that have units that specialize in treating eating disorders. Choose one that includes intensive psychotherapy. The organizations listed in the Resources section can help you locate such facilities in your area.

Avoid facilities that are considered weight loss centers or spas. These programs are not as interested in the emotional well-being of their clients as they are in weight loss. They are not the place for someone who is physically ill, nor are they the answer for treatment of severe eating disorders.

Inpatient care is a serious interruption to one's life. It can involve anywhere from several weeks to many months and should not be undertaken lightly. If someone must be hospitalized, it should be in a facility that provides both psychological and physiological services, and should be pursued only after competent professionals agree that the benefits of hospitalization outweigh its potentially disruptive aspects.

Intensive Outpatient Programs

One alternative to hospitalization is the intensive outpatient program (IOP). IOPs allow for a more concentrated level of care without the need to leave one's day-to-day life completely. Programs are usually held five days a week for eight hours daily. One or two meals are served during that time as part of the treatment itself. Some IOP programs are held just during the evening, allowing patients to continue working or attending school, but providing intensive treatment during the dinner and evening hours when concerns about eating may be most pronounced.

IOPs can be used effectively when someone is in need of direct intervention with the symptom but does not want to disrupt her daily life by entering a hospital. They are also used as a means of making a smooth transition from the safety of a hospital to engagement in the outside world. They can allow treatment to continue when inpatient stays are terminated due to limited insurance coverage. Or they may be incorporated as an adjunct to outpatient therapy when the patient feels stuck in treatment (and is perhaps retreating to disturbed eating behavior), and she needs the intensive focus of an ongoing program to examine what is wrong.

In IOPs, patients are seen in a structured program that focuses on symptom management and psychological understanding of the eating disorder. Therapy usually consists of group treatment, and meals are attended (often lunch and/or dinner) as part of the treatment program. Helping the patient abate starving, bingeing, and/or purging is a critical aspect of these programs.

Participation in IOPs can last from one or two weeks to several months, depending on the needs of the person involved.

Managed Care and Patient Advocacy

In recent years, managed care has become the system that organizes and directs health care for a growing percentage of people. When this is the case, in order to receive coverage, the patient usually must seek treatment from a participating health care provider who is part of the managed care program. The patient is given a list of names of specialists who can meet one's health care needs. Additionally, the health care program determines how long treatment is needed. Thus outpatient therapies and hospitalizations are directly affected by the insurance companies' assessments.

For example, before managed care, if a patient were hospitalized, the patient and doctors determined how long inpatient care should last. Now, for the most part, managed care allows approximately two weeks for the hospitalization of an eating-disordered patient. It is important to note, however, that at the onset of hospitalization, the insurance companies and the hospitals cannot guarantee how long coverage will last. Once the person is an inpatient, the hospital or residential care facility negotiates with the insurance companies for length of stay. The extent of depression or other symptoms secondary to the eating disorder may often be determining factors in assessment of coverage. Inpatient facilities will do all they can to prolong the length of stay if they feel it is needed, but insurance companies do not always accede to these recommendations. When this is the case, hospitals and residential care programs will usually recommend IOP programs, so that treatment is continued, despite the interruptions.

When managed care is directing treatment choices, it is important that the patient and family do not relinquish their roles in treatment planning. If you are assigned a health care provider by your insurance company, it is still critical to evaluate him or her. As with out-of-network professionals, see if anyone you know is familiar with any of the professionals on the provider list. The patient or parent still has the right to interview different providers and to have a say in which therapist or doctor will be chosen.

For the most part, managed care administrators are interested in symptom abatement and less concerned with the treatment of underlying factors that cause and maintain symptoms. Thus, at times, the insurance company may stop coverage even though the patient may still be in need of treatment.

In these cases, there are some things that patients or families can do to gain the cooperation of the managed care company. Do not leave reimbursement only in the hands of the insurance company or doctor. Get involved. Find out the name of the case manager who is evaluating the claim. Tell the case manager about the person seeking the claim. Talk about why treatment coverage should be extended or why someone out of network should be covered. Sometimes this allows the case manager to know the claimant as a person and not just as a number, and this can affect reimbursement.

Sometimes the insurance plan will not cover the desired treatment. If this is the case, don't lose hope. Limitations of coverage for one type of treatment may not apply to others. For example, some health care companies will pay for only a week or two of hospitalization, but they will continue coverage for treatment in an intensive outpatient program. Additionally, some outpatient facilities offer low-cost treatment as an alternative to using insurance coverage. There are many free support groups as well. Sometimes, however, there are no low-cost options and no possibility of reimbursement. This is the reality of today's health care system, and there is no minimizing the pain that this causes for many families. When that is the case, be sure to speak to others in your situation. Not only can that be an invaluable source of support, but mutual brainstorming may allow for treatment options that have yet to be considered.

Finding the Services That Are Needed

There may be times when you are in the position of helping the person you care about find the professional services that she needs, whether managed care is involved or not.

The ideal way to find good professional help is through personal recommendation. If you're looking for a psychotherapist, for example, you might ask your doctor, a school counselor, or a teacher whom he or she would send a daughter to if she had this problem. Friends and relatives may also be good sources of information.

Perhaps you know people who are in or have been in treatment (even for problems other than eating disorders). Ask if they are satisfied and would recommend the person they are seeing. This therapist may not be experienced with eating disorders or may not want to work with a friend or acquaintance of a client, but he or she will likely be able to recommend a therapist who can help with eating disorders.

You might also seek out facilities, such as teaching hospitals or outpatient psychotherapy centers, in your area that specialize in the treatment of eating disorders. They will have the names of therapists and other medical specialists. Or contact one of the programs listed in the Resources section of this book. They will be able to help you locate specialists and eating-disorder treatment facilities in your geographic location

The National Association of Anorexia Nervosa and Associated Disorders (ANAD) has been extremely effective in establishing support groups throughout the world. If you are looking for a support group (or are interested in starting one), contact them directly.

Choosing a Therapist

If you are helping someone look for a therapist or choosing one for yourself or your family, the process of a consultation is the best one we know of to evaluate a particular therapist. There are certain questions that are useful for people entering therapy to ask at the outset. As a parent arranging therapy for a minor, you may be in the position of asking these questions yourself, either on the phone or during a consultation with the therapist.

Questions for All Therapists

1. *Ask about credentials.* Choose a qualified practitioner who is licensed (or training toward licensure) in his or her respective discipline. Most therapists are trained as psychologists, psychiatrists, or social workers. Licensing and credential requirements vary from state to state. Be sure the person you're meeting with either is in the process of being licensed or is already licensed. This in and of itself does not guarantee good training and high ethics, but it is a start.

2. *Ask about the therapist's experience and views about treatment.* A specialization in the area of eating disorders is very important. You want to be sure the therapist has a compassionate view of the symptom, that he or she knows the eating behavior is related to attempts at coping with inner emotional difficulties such as problems of identity, conflicts, and maturation. You will want someone who will work specifically with changing the symptom while at the same time developing an understanding of why the symptom may be needed in one's life. You want to stay clear of people who view eating disorders as a lack of willpower or bad eating habits.

   If the person or family entering therapy has addictions other than food (that is, alcoholism or drug abuse), you will want to make sure that the professional is knowledgeable about and experienced in the area of addictions, is informed about and supportive of Alcoholics Anonymous or similar support networks, and is capable of dealing directly with these other addictions in addition to the eating disorder.

3. *Find out how much treatment will cost.* You will find a vast range in fees depending on the type of services being sought. Most likely fees will be higher for private practitioners than for clinic facilities.

4. *Inquire as to billing procedures.* Is payment required each session or once a month?

5. *Find out the policy on missed sessions.* Many therapists charge for missed sessions. Can these appointments be rescheduled? Is the patient charged for vacations? In particular, if you are a parent paying for your child's individual or group therapy, will you be informed if she misses sessions? Parents and therapists have different preferences in this regard. Be sure you understand the policy before your daughter begins therapy so there won't be misunderstandings later on.

6. *Find out about insurance reimbursement.* If the person in treatment has health insurance, check the policy to see what coverage is possible.
   A therapist must be licensed in order for insurance reimbursement to be considered. Licensing involves passing a state licensing exam, practicing for a certain number of years, and maintaining good ethical standing in the professional community. Be aware that not all professionals take insurance reimbursement as direct payment for services.
   If you are using a health care provider from a managed care program, coverage may be possible only if the therapist is a provider in the insurance plan's health care network. Be sure you understand the terms of the insurance coverage, whether services for a therapist out of network will be covered, and at what point reimbursement might be terminated.

7. *Find out the policy on family members' involvement.* With adolescents or even with young adults who are supported financially, parents need to know what their role is going to be with regard

to treatment and the food itself. Should they actively be involved in feeding their daughter? Will they be seen in adjunct sessions with their daughter? Can they call the therapist if they are concerned about how things are going? No parent should be expected to back out of treatment completely. However, therapists have different positions with all of these questions, and the role parents should take will vary tremendously in each situation. Be sure from the outset that you know what the arrangement is, why it is set up that way, and how your questions and concerns can be addressed as treatment progresses.

8. *Discuss what will happen in a crisis.* If you're arranging treatment for an adolescent, you might want to know how the therapist handles a crisis situation. There are some situations in which you *must* be contacted by the therapist. For example, if the client is suicidal and a minor, parents should be alerted; in the case of a married client, the husband should be called. There are some situations, however, that are more ambiguous. What if your 19-year-old daughter is taking drugs? What if an adolescent is pregnant? If you are the parents of a minor, you have a right to be contacted in certain types of situations in which your child may be in trouble. If you are a parent of someone older, or a husband or friend, your rights are less clear (even if you are paying for the therapy). At the start of therapy, discuss with the therapist how crises are handled and in what types of situations (if any) you will be contacted.

There are other questions that may be useful depending on the type of therapy pursued.

Evaluating the Therapist

One question that is frequently asked of all types of therapists is whether it is beneficial to have a therapist who has been eating disordered herself or himself. This is not necessary. What is most important is for the therapist to have the empathy to feel for and understand the patient's experience. Psychotherapists do not need to have experienced myriad emotional problems from anxiety to depression to phobias to be helpful in treating these disturbances. Indeed, it would be impossible to have experienced everything that one treats. In this regard, psychotherapy is not unlike medicine. If you are a doctor, you don't need to have had cancer in order to treat it.

Because someone has been eating disordered does not guarantee that he or she will be more understanding of the patient's experience. Sometimes a therapist is still so close to his or her own personal struggle with food that the therapist insists on seeing the patient's difficulties as similar to his or her own when that might not be the case. In any therapeutic situation, it is important that the therapist be free to understand the patient's personal experience and not color it by thinking it similar to what he or she has gone through.

Regardless of whether a therapist is or is not eating disordered, it is also unlikely that he or she will tell you. Therapists do not usually share intimate details of their own history. Such information can be a burden to the patient.

What you or the patient should be concerned with is the therapist's training in the area of eating disorders, experience with patients, and sensitivity to people. These are perhaps the most valuable qualities to look for in a therapist. A personal experience with an eating disorder is never a substitute for rigorous education and training.

A Good Match

Sometimes it is a good idea for the eating-disordered person to have consultations with a few different people. This can provide the feel of how different people work. It is important that the match between therapist and patient be a good one. A patient needs to feel she can trust this person. It is, after all, going to be a long and hard journey together; the more comfortable she is at the outset, the more likely she will be able to stick with it during the more difficult moments of treatment, and thus the more effective her therapy will be.

In your search, don't minimize the reality of finances. Sometimes, in an attempt to get the "best" treatment, families or patients meet with someone they can't afford, hoping that the therapist's experience will result in a shorter length of treatment. While there is no minimizing the importance of a therapist's expertise, even with the most seasoned therapists, treatment can be a long and complicated process. Only enter into a situation that you can afford to continue for an unspecified period of time. Otherwise the pressure for the treatment to "work" and be finished can actually thwart the work that needs to be done.

When It's a Poor Match

It is not uncommon for a patient to feel unsure about a therapist in the beginning of treatment. The new patient doesn't know much about the therapist and needs time to build trust. But sometimes the relationship just may not be a good match. All too often, patients assume that discomfort about therapy is part of their problem. Feelings of discomfort or mistrust should not be negated. One's own intuition can be a useful resource and should be respected.

Usually the best bet is to give the therapy at least two or three sessions before a decision to leave is made. During this time, the patient should tell the therapist about her uneasiness. Sometimes voicing these apprehensions allows for a discussion that can abate the discomfort. If this doesn't happen, however, and mistrust or uneasiness continues, a consultation with someone else is in order.

The person in therapy needs to know that it is okay to leave. The therapist should be told what is wrong and why it makes sense to move on. Some therapists may want to meet one or more additional times to see if anything can be changed or to have a chance to end the relationship comfortably. This is common practice. But if the person in therapy is unhappy, endings should not drag on too long.

What to Expect from Treatment

How Long Will It Take?

Once someone has found a therapist she likes, this is often the start of a long process toward recovery. The most frequent question we are asked is, How long will it take? Unfortunately, this is also one of the hardest to answer. The time it takes depends on many factors.

The duration of the eating disorder will certainly be a determining factor: The shorter its history, the more likely and more quickly recovery is possible. A 14-year-old who has been bulimic for under a year is more likely to benefit from therapy than a 30-year-old who has been bulimic since her college days. This does *not* mean that therapy will be ineffective for the 30-year-old, but it will most likely take longer before an abatement in the symptoms is seen. The severity of the problem is also a big factor. Some people, for example, vomit once or twice a week after having a big meal. Others spend most of their waking hours eating and getting rid of food. For this latter group, the eating disorder is a much more active part of one's daily life, and in these situations it will obviously take a much longer time.

Other addictions, such as drug or alcohol dependency, other psychological problems, or difficulties in the family (such as substance abuse, incest, or domestic problems), will add to the complications and therefore the length of therapy.

Change takes time. An entrenched eating disorder is a very serious condition, and treatment typically involves years, not months. Some people expect that when the eating disturbance goes away, psychotherapy is over. This is not true. The process of psychotherapy helps people resolve the emotional dilemmas that led them to food in the first place. This process only fully begins when the eating itself is less of an issue. When someone is in treatment, she needs to develop her own pace of recovery.

What Behavior Changes Can You Expect to See?

When someone enters therapy, the main goal of treatment is indeed change in the disordered eating and thinking. That being said, how and when these changes occur should be evaluated differently depending on the actual eating disorder and the severity of the problem.

For example, if someone has a long history of binge eating or bulimic behavior, the eating disorder may not lessen in a predictable manner. Sometimes, the bingeing or purging actually increases at first in a last-ditch attempt to hold onto the behavior before someone has to give it up. In other situations, self-destructive eating patterns stop immediately, only to begin again once the person starts to feel emotions she has kept hidden for years. In yet other situations, the bingeing or purging can fluctuate on and off for years before there is lasting change.

With bulimia or binge eating, the benefits of therapy cannot solely be measured on the basis of changes in the eating disorder itself. Sometimes quick improvements in the eating patterns are short-lived, prompted by a display of "white-knuckle" willpower or a wish to please the therapist. Developing a trusting relationship, expressing feelings, and increasing one's self-esteem have to be established before a more sustained change in the eating can occur. These less observable changes are crucial as a basis of long-term growth.

With the anorexic patient, however, the initial goals of treatment are much different. Here, because of the life-threatening aspects of the disorder, change in eating and weight need to be seen much more quickly. Someone who is anorexic needs to be monitored by a physician (and often a nutritionist) as well as a therapist, and weekly weigh-ins should be a required part of the treatment. Here, one can expect that a slow but progressive increase in eating and weight should occur in order for outpatient treatment to continue.

Regardless of whether parents are actively engaged in refeeding their daughter or not, they certainly need to be informed on an ongoing basis about how treatment is progressing and whether weight is being gained. Sometimes the therapist, doctor, and patient agree that parents don't need to know the actual weight itself, as revealing it can be humiliating for the patient and can undermine the progress. Indeed, because the number on the scale itself is so frightening to the anorexic, it is not uncommon for the patient to be weighed "blind" and not informed of her actual weight. But everyone involved, parents included, do need to know whether that number is increasing, decreasing, or staying the same.

If the eating is not changed, and weight is not at least steadied in the first couple of weeks, you, as a parent, will have to intervene and assess what needs to be done next. In this case, the first order of business is to speak with the therapist directly and see if there is a clear plan of action as to how to proceed. If the therapist won't speak to you, or if you have questions that remain, a consultation with another professional with expertise in anorexia may well be in order.

What Mood Changes Can You Expect to See?

"The first year of Katrina's therapy was hell," Grace and Jim Williams told us about their 16-year-old daughter, who had had a long history of binge eating.

> We expected that once she was in therapy, things would get better. But it didn't go that way. It was unclear what Katrina was doing with her eating. Sometimes she ate really healthfully—and then the next minute food would be missing and it was obvious to all of us that she was secretly bingeing again. But even worse, she became a complete misery to be around. Suddenly, she decided it was okay to tell everyone what she thought of them; going way beyond being honest, she was really nasty. Her moods were intolerable—one day sullen, one day angry. We just wanted to stay out of her way. Things got a lot better after the first year, but that beginning time was horrible.

Katrina's family's experience differed from that of Alice's, an 18-year-old bulimic. Alice's parents told us that when Alice started to see someone, it was as though a black cloud had been lifted from the whole family: "Her mood brightened. She was visibly relieved, which made us all feel better."

There is no way of predicting how therapy will affect someone. It is a time when new behaviors will be attempted, new emotions will come to the surface. If you are not in a life-threatening situation, such as that with an anorexic, don't rush to make judgments.

How to Be Helpful

How to be most helpful to someone in treatment will vary from person to person. One 24-year-old woman, Jacki, told us that she felt bad that her parents never asked how she was doing in therapy. It made her feel shameful about going, as if this were an embarrassment to everyone. Her parents, on the other hand, wanted to know how she was doing, but they were afraid that if they asked, Jacki would get angry. (It wouldn't be the first time they had been told to mind their own business.) So Jacki and her parents silently misunderstood one another and were uncomfortable whenever they did get together.

If someone you know is entering therapy, ask her how involved she'd like you to be. Can you ask her how she's doing? What should you do if you're worried? Should you contact the therapist? Discuss your feelings openly, and be willing to accept whatever answer the person in therapy gives you. This will certainly ease the discomfort often felt when someone you care about enters therapy. Together, the two of you can anticipate how you'd like to handle potential difficult spots before they arise.

When You're Not Sure About the Progress of Therapy

As with Grace and Jim Williams, it is sometimes hard to believe that therapy is doing any good for the person you know. Perhaps she is upset, still eating disordered, and seems no better than before.

Depending on the severity of the situation at hand, your role will vary. No question, if your daughter is anorexic and there is no forward movement with eating or weight, you need to intervene and speak with the therapist and treatment team regarding initial treatment goals. This would also be the case if your daughter is severely symptomatic in other ways, such as daily bingeing or purging, with no change at all in the symptoms.

No matter what your concern, the first thing to do is to ask your daughter how therapy is going. She might tell you that she is happy with her therapist and that she feels like she is moving forward. However, if you are concerned that the disordered eating is not changing at all, you should tell her that you are worried and that you need to let the therapist know your concerns. Often the therapist will hear you out but may not be able to respond directly. Regardless of the privacy that may be needed in an individual therapy, if your daughter is underage or financially supported by you, there should be an opportunity for you to know what to expect in the treatment and what role you should be playing with the eating disorder. If your concerns are not addressed, insist on a meeting with the therapist and your daughter, or see another professional for a second opinion. In particular, if you are concerned about someone who is anorexic and weight loss continues, you must be able to speak with the therapist to understand what needs to be done next.

The therapist should have a clear plan of action regarding symptomatic behavior. He or she should be able to explain clearly why treatment should continue and what goals are currently being met. In more severe situations, the therapist should have a plan that involves the need for more intensive treatment if symptoms don't abate.

However, the therapist may explain that, as long as your daughter is medically stable and a treatment plan is developed, the work may be slow, and the symptoms may not change as rapidly as one would like. In these situations, it might be best to pull back and not force the issue. The door should be left open to speak with the therapist and your daughter to reassess the situation as treatment progresses. But at this point, it is not the time to insist on a change in therapy. In fact, if you're paying for the therapy, you should anticipate this possibility beforehand and be prepared that even though *you* may not like the results, if the person in therapy and the treatment team are encouraged, at least in the initial phases of treatment, it is important not to interfere. Often the changes that occur are subtle at first and will be much more noticeable to the person in therapy than to anyone observing her. If you continue to remain concerned, however, a second opinion with a professional well experienced with eating disorders may be in order.

For some proportion of eating-disordered people, therapy is not going to help with the eating disorder. In fact, treatment follow-up studies indicate, sadly, that approximately one third of anorexic and bulimic patients remain unchanged symptomatically, despite clinical and psychopharmacological interventions.[20] The recidivism rate for binge eating is even higher. If your daughter has been in multiple therapies or hospitalized several times with no change in the eating disorder, you may be facing this kind of poignant situation. Certainly, it is imperative that you speak with the therapist and perhaps have a second opinion regarding treatment goals.

In these cases, despite a lack of progress with the symptoms, the goal is to use therapy to enhance the quality of the person's life, despite the ongoing presence of disordered eating and weight. Here, if the person indicates that the treatment is beneficial, it is important to encourage her to continue. As upsetting and exasperating as it is if someone does not change an eating disorder, it is possible nonetheless for someone to carve out a full life for herself. Therapy can help pave the way for other life goals to be reached despite the ongoing struggle with food and weight.

What If No Therapist Is the Right One?

Sometimes, no therapy ever seems to progress. Someone may jump from therapist to therapist, program to program, disappointed that no one can help. Sometimes these individuals have a very deep sense of dissatisfaction with everything and everyone around them. They are overwhelmed by their own pain, and if they go to a therapist, it is with the hope for a process that is swift and painless—a "magical solution" to the problem.

Therapy, however, is not magical. The process of developing a relationship with a therapist can be difficult and anxiety-ridden, especially for people who have little capacity to trust others. The process of knowing themselves better can be frightening and foreign, and they resist it at every turn. No matter what type of treatment is ultimately undertaken, there must be a commitment on the patient's part to the work. When the patient cannot make this commitment, the therapy will not succeed.

But even when the commitment is made, for reasons no one quite understands yet, some people just cannot be reached by the therapy process, multiple hospitalizations, and inevitably different courses of medication. They continue on a chronic course of disturbed eating. Problems will likely exist in many areas of their lives, and therapy will not be of much help.

For relatives and friends, these situations are most difficult. The helplessness and frustration that this type of situation engenders are enormous. No matter how severe the situation, there is nothing anyone can do to make a person stick with or benefit from therapy. Hospitalization can be used if the situation becomes an emergency, but you cannot force someone to change.

It is a terrible experience to watch someone you care about suffer and know there is nothing you can do. Your life inevitably has been relentlessly changed, and a sense of loss as to what could have been pervades. If you are facing such a crisis, you must get support and not go it alone. It is time for you to seek help for yourself.

What About You? Taking Care of Yourself

Whether your situation is as critical as just described, or whether your concerns feel minor by contrast, you are still going to be left with questions, concerns, and fears of your own. If the person is not in treatment, and you're not sure if a serious problem exists, read Chapters 4 and 5, and consider consulting a professional or group. However, regardless of whether someone is or is not in treatment, having to accept the reality of the problem, the limitations of what you can do, and the limitations of what you can expect from therapy can leave you frightened, angry, and worried. You will need a place to voice your concerns and to learn how to make an independent life for yourself. You will need support regarding how to deal with eating issues as they arise. Perhaps you may be confused as to how to respond to the messages you are given by that person as she changes. Or you might be struggling with serious life problems and/or addictions of your own. We have found it invaluable for parents, spouses, even friends, at times, to meet with a therapist themselves or to join a support group for significant others.

Therapy

The most important goal when dealing with someone who has an eating disorder is to help that person grow and change so that she can be more responsible for her own self-care. Often that means examining your relationship to understand what effect the eating disorder has had on your life, what role you should take at this stage, and, just as importantly, what rules need questioning so that everyone in the relationship is able to better communicate, connect, and develop as individuals.

It is very common for the parents and spouses of eating-disordered people to find that they have somehow become dependent on the symptomatic person and her behavior. Brenda Jones, for example, noticed that when Wendy, her 16-year-old anorexic daughter, recovered, it was hard for her and her husband to go back to what their life had been before Wendy's illness. Their marriage had revolved around Wendy. Now that she was going about her life, the Joneses had to work hard to rebuild their relationship. Brenda spoke about it this way:

> We hadn't talked about anything but Wendy or done anything but worry about her for so long. In therapy, we were given assignments to spend time together talking about anything but our daughter. Because we'd been so involved with Wendy, it took an "outsider" to remind us that our own marriage was being neglected. The therapist was able to suggest specific things we could do that would help us be a couple again, not just parents.

Support Groups

Most parents we meet initially don't want to speak to other parents about their own situation. They feel embarrassed, filled with a sense of failure or defeat. Yet parental support can be enormously helpful and educational. A support group can also help you feel less alone with the problems you encounter as the other person goes through the process of recovery.

The Resources listed at the back of the book can help you locate parental support groups in your area. If there are none available, the organizations listed will help you establish one. Almost every parent has told us the same thing—that once they do speak with others, there is something comforting and almost always directly helpful when they hear others' experiences regarding the daily challenges that inevitably arise.

Information and Education

There are newsletters and online mailings from various organizations that are available to keep you aware of up-to-date information. Not only is such information educational, but it also provides a forum of ideas and experiences and can keep you from feeling isolated. There are now national hotlines that you or the eating-disordered person can call for help as well as multiple chat rooms to discuss your particular concerns. Use the Resources list to find the information you need.

Part III

Using New Strategies

7

What to Do About the Problems with Food

Practical Advice for Disengaging from the Food Fights

When someone you care about has an eating disorder, regardless of whether or not she is in treatment, you are bound to have questions regarding how to handle food and weight issues. For example, what should you do about her binges? If she's refusing to eat, should you make her eat? Should you say anything if you think she's gaining too much weight? Who should do the shopping?

Interventions to change someone else's eating are appropriate only as part of a well thought out treatment plan under the guidance of a therapist. Except in these closely monitored circumstances, as part of a larger therapeutic picture, attempts at changing someone's eating almost *never* work. They usually result in relentless control battles. Or, in families, one parent insists on change, while the other gives up, creating burdensome tensions among everyone involved. When the sufferer's own motivation is not encouraged, you will find that when your control lets up, she returns to the problematic behaviors.

This chapter offers practical advice about what you should do regarding the bingeing, starving, purging, and obsessions with weight that you are confronted with on a daily basis. The approach offered encourages you to disentangle yourself from the problems with food and to engage with the person in ways that will encourage her to become responsible for her actions and the consequences of her behavior. She is then free to make lasting changes in her behavior and in her relationships. This approach is needed even when you are actively refeeding a low-weight anorexic. There are times when you will be actively involved with the food. But there will also be, on a day-to-day basis, a myriad of situations in which you need to unemotionally disengage from the struggle and focus on helping your daughter take care of herself. No matter what the specifics of your particular situation, the strategies discussed will help you to encourage change while minimizing the destructive impact of the eating disorder on your relationship, your life, and your living situation. The work that needs to be done is part of a broader process, often undertaken with the guidance of a therapist or support group.

The goal is not merely to allow someone to regain a healthy relationship with food, but to use the eating disorder as an opportunity for the family to grow and change in whatever ways are needed at that particular time.

Living Healthfully

Parents ask us all the time whether their attempts to eat well and look trim have caused their child to develop an eating disorder. Parents who eat healthfully and exercise regularly in fact can be good role models for the person struggling with bingeing, starving, or compulsive exercise. In and of themselves, these activities do not cause an eating disorder.

Problems develop not from setting a healthy example, but from insisting that someone follow it in a way that doesn't allow for individual differences. Parents can set a good example, but children have to have choices as well. This is true for the overweight child, where a "no sweets" rule can lead to more trouble, not less. A better alternative would be to have a rule in which kids are allowed to choose when they will eat sweets, and what the sweets will be, even if a limit is placed on how much. This is also true in a different way for the starving anorexic. For example, she may not have a choice about having to eat breakfast, but she may be able to decide whether she is going to have an egg or yogurt for her meal.

Getting Perspective

"My daughter, Migelle, has always been heavy, ever since she was a child," Jamie Canton said of her 12-year-old daughter.

> *My husband, John, and I eat so well—we don't understand why she has such a hard time following the examples we set. We would have organic food and fruit in the house all the time.*
>
> *We finally spoke to a therapist instead of a diet doctor, and we were told that Migelle should be able to have two "fun" things a day to eat and that it was up to her to eat them when she wanted to. At first, it made me crazy—Migelle would eat breakfast and then sit down to eat a piece of pie and a cookie. But something about her knowing that how she ate was her choice seemed to help. In the last months, she has eaten more healthfully than I have ever seen previously. She has lost 5 of the 20 pounds*

the doctor told her to lose, but more importantly, she seems happy for the
first time in a very long time.

In order to be able to disentangle yourself from the food issues, you must accept your own limitations. Even if you are directly feeding your daughter with the help of a professional, you can set a structure and guidelines, but within that framework, it will rarely look like what you had hoped. It is a part of the recovery process that you let go of your own ideas of how the person should be and realistically assess who she is, what she is capable of doing, and what kind of help she needs in order to take hold of her own life. This is where it is important to remember that even when you are refeeding your child, the goal is not to control her. You are establishing a framework that will allow her to ultimately change herself. In some situations, more active intervention will be needed on your part. In other situations, you will need to back off. In either case, you are providing the groundwork so that her needs are heard, both by others and by herself. You are not merely making someone change. This is a subtle but critical difference. The person you *can* change is *you*. In this chapter we show you how.

Rule 1: Accept your limitations.

Michael and Melissa Fine are both successful lawyers in their forties. They are accustomed to success. They were taught that if you really want something, nothing should get in your way. When their 16-year-old daughter, Sherrie, became bulimic, it was the one thing they couldn't conquer, and it drove them crazy. For the first time in their lives they felt like failures. Michael put it this way:

Melissa and I decided the best way for us both to have exciting careers and still have a family was to have only one child. After Sherrie was born, we were still able to travel and enjoy all the same things we'd done before.

We took on parenting the way we did everything—with all our energy. We spent hours with Sherrie when she was little, helping her develop every skill we considered important. When Sherrie started school, she was the brightest and best student. Melissa and I helped her with her homework, her science projects, her book reports. Our home was the hangout for all Sherrie's friends. When she was older and had trouble with a boyfriend, we would talk and help her figure out a solution to the problem.

Sherrie's becoming bulimic was the biggest shock of our lives. But we'd weathered lots of other things; Melissa and I could handle this too. Boy, were we wrong! I'm ashamed to think now how long we tried to take care of the bulimia ourselves. We developed food regimens and bathroom schedules and made it the focus of our lives. The more time we spent on trying to control Sherrie's bingeing and purging, the worse it got.

Finally, we went to therapy. It's hard for Melissa and me to give up on the idea that we can't control Sherrie's eating. It's difficult for us to not feel like failures.

Rule 2: Accept the other person's right to be different from you.

Jonathan and Caroline Eldridge knew that they had to intervene when their 14-year-old daughter, Carrie, almost stopped eating completely. What had started out as a normal diet to lose a few pounds had catapulted into full-fledged anorexia, and within four months, Carrie, who was already five feet, six inches, had steadily lost almost 20 pounds. It became clear as well that she had stopped menstruating. Her parents tried to actively intervene with awards and punishments for eating behavior. They talked, they lectured, they tried to understand. But when nothing intervened, and a forced doctor's visit showed a weight of 105, the Eldridges engaged a family therapist to help them better take hold of their daughter's crisis with food.

In fact, with a team of therapists and physicians at their side, Jonathan and Caroline were able to help Carrie begin to eat more. Carrie's weight edged up to 110, but there she stood firm. No matter what anyone did, no matter the therapeutic interventions, parental limits, or cajoling, Carrie had had enough. The Eldridges were in a bind. Carrie was now eating on her own, maintaining her weight, and actively reengaged in school and with friends. She was hardly at a weight that would warrant hospitalization. However, this weight was not enough to reinstate her lost menstrual cycle, and everyone but Carrie was worried.

"What we had to realize," Jonathan said, speaking for himself and his wife, "was that Carrie was in the right direction and needed some time to catch her breath. When we tried to intervene, we started to lose her again—she ate less, isolated herself, basically got enraged. This was actually harder than when we first thought she might be hospitalized. What we had to accept was that it wasn't going to go exactly as we had hoped and that it was time to back off and give Carrie a chance to see what she would do next."

Six months later, Carrie's weight had actually inched up another two pounds. While she still was not menstruating, the team and parents had agreed that Carrie was moving in the right direction and needed to be recognized and supported in her efforts. Everyone, including Carrie, agreed that with ongoing therapy and doctor visits in place, as long as no more weight was lost, Carrie could be in charge of her eating for the rest of the year. At that time (in six months), the situation could be reevaluated to determine what, if anything, needed to be done next.

These kinds of decisions, which often involve health issues, are extremely complicated and laden with many fears (usually more fears for the parents than the person with the eating disorder). While the goal is always to reinstate full healthy development, it is critical at these times to keep in mind that slowing down the process and accepting one's own limits, instead of reinstating a control battle, may achieve the much bigger goal of ultimately encouraging self-care.

Until you can accept rules 1 and 2, you will not be able to disengage from the eating problem sufficiently for change to take place. John and Mary Brown were unable to pull out of their daughter Tracey's struggle with bulimia. When Tracey's therapist told them to leave Tracey's eating to her, the Browns were not pleased. "If she would just make up her mind to stop, she could. She's being stubborn," said John to the therapist. Mary worked hard to get Tracey to stop, hoping to calm John's annoyance.

The idea that the bulimia was more powerful than Tracey's willpower was contrary to the family's values. John had made it professionally as a successful attorney after an impoverished childhood. He put himself through law school at night while working days. Mary raised her three daughters and then went back to teaching, the profession she had left to marry and raise her family. The Browns had overcome many obstacles in their lives, and they saw Tracey's problem as resulting from a lack of self-control. They were determined to help her in the ways they believed would work.

No matter how many times they were prevailed upon to leave the problem to Tracey, they could not let it go. There always seemed to be another strategy they hadn't tried. John felt that if they persisted, they could get Tracey to stop. The Browns could not accept their powerlessness in this situation.

Tracey dropped out of treatment and tried hard to cooperate with her parents' attempts to help her. This went on for years, and the Browns remain entangled in Tracey's problems.

Tracey lives on her own now, but she talks to her parents daily about her eating habits. She lets them know when she's had "good days" and when she's had "bad days." Tracey's eating problem has remained the focus in her relationship with her parents—a focus that prevents both sides from separating and growing.

In another family, the Johnsons, Maggie Johnson's ability to change her behavior allowed her daughter, Sarah, the room to take charge of her own eating, with much better results.

Maggie's response to her daughter's confession of vomiting was to take Sarah to their physician and then to the therapist he recommended for evaluation. Maggie was not unaccustomed to tough times. Having been left by her husband when Sarah was a year and a half old, she was used to working hard at achieving the comforts she and Sarah enjoyed. The daughter of an alcoholic mother, Maggie knew independence and survival from an early age. Her strong commitment and sense of responsibility were qualities that she had relied on throughout her life. She used these in dealing with Sarah's problems now. Sarah's therapist told Maggie to leave all food decisions up to Sarah herself. That turned out to be much easier said than done, as Maggie quickly found out.

I'm used to doing things, not not doing things, as Sarah's doctor requested. Sarah is 16, and I felt she needed me. It was a long, hard struggle to realize she needed me in a different way than telling her what to eat and ensuring she wouldn't vomit. I had to learn to trust Sarah, not that she wouldn't binge, but to deal with this particular behavior in her own way. I had to have faith that I had instilled in her enough strength to fight the battle on her own—and win! The only way to let her know I believed she could do it was to let her do it.

In time, Maggie's faith in her own capacities allowed her to believe in Sarah's. "Of course I still worry," she said. "How can I stop? But with the help of friends and family, I was able to leave Sarah alone to get a grip on her bulimia."

Parents' roles with eating-disordered teenagers are endlessly complicated. In general, we have found that in order to get well, the person with the eating disorder needs to be able to make decisions about her food intake and weight. However, that does not mean that she is making all the decisions or that the parents should not be involved.

With anorexia, what works best, whether parents are involved in refeeding or not, is when there is a clear path of consequences, no matter what the situation. For example, with an anorexic who is at a low but not critical weight (and a doctor has determined that she can still go to school and be treated on an outpatient basis), a minimal but steady weight gain must be achieved each week. A doctor or nutritionist should assess the weight weekly, and if the goal isn't reached, a valued activity, such as dance or sports, should be taken away. If the person is at a lower weight, it may mean that a pound a week is gained, or the person goes into the hospital. There does not have to be fighting, emotional scenes, or ongoing control battles—just clear consequences, with a team of professionals in place to support parents in setting limits and helping the teenager to move forward. With someone who is bulimic or a binge eater, the goal will not be about weight gain or even stopping the bingeing or purging (because that may take some time). But it may be that the person has to attend weekly sessions with a therapist, or consequences will be set up.

The point here is not that of punishment—or even control. The point is to assess how you as parents can maintain a position of gentle but clear authority and how your daughter can best be guided to envision her life as her own. Thus, even if options are limited (eating breakfast or going to a hospital as an extreme but not unfamiliar example), it still becomes her choice as to what she will do next.

Of course, this is never as straightforward as it sounds. Usually it means that if the desired goal isn't met (the weekly pound isn't gained, for example), the person has a couple more days to try again. But consequences are clearly spelled out and in place, so that if the person can't achieve her goals in the days to follow, the next steps are ready to be put into action (for example, the coach knows that the next swim meet will not be attended, or an appropriate hospital has already been contacted and admission is possible).

It is important to note that when dealing with a child or teen who has put on weight due to binge eating, just setting consequences or rewards for weight loss will likely result in control battles and sneak eating. For example, when a teen is morbidly obese, it may well mean that she has to lose a pound weekly (in the care of a physician), or more intensive care is warranted. With a teenager whose bingeing is not significantly interfering with her health or her life, this would likely not be the treatment of choice. Be sure to consult with a professional before considering what goals and consequences are best for your particular child.

What is important is that the person with the eating disorder is given responsibility for her life, no matter how sick she may be. Goals are set, limits are established, and the message is unemotional and clear: there are different consequences for different behaviors. It is up to the person, no matter the age, no matter the eating disorder, to decide how she is going to proceed.

Cathy, a 14-year-old anorexic just out of a two-week inpatient facility, was hovering at five feet, four inches and 95 pounds. She knew if she lost one more pound she would be placed back in an inpatient program. She was scared and determined not to go back to a hospital but described mealtimes this way:

> *I know what I have to do, but I sit at the table, and I just can't get myself to eat. In my head, I hear voices saying, "You are a pig. You are going to get fat. You will be heavier than anyone else who's come out of the hospital program." My parents go crazy. They start to plead with me to eat. That only makes things worse. First I'm in a fight in my head—and then I'm in a fight with them because I just want them to be quiet.*
>
> *If I'm going to even take a bite, it has to be because I've dared myself to do it—to just take one step into the water. The second I hear my parents' voices, I just shut down.*

The first time out of the hospital, Cathy let the voices in her head win. At 94 pounds, as her parents and the team had decided, she was readmitted into the inpatient facility. The next time around (and it's never clear why, but certainly she knew her parents meant business), she hovered at 99 pounds, never breaking the dreaded three-digit mark—but then again, never landing back in the hospital.

In the following pages we offer new strategies for you to try. We apply rules 1 and 2 to the areas of daily living that seem to be the most problematic in dealing with someone who has an eating disorder: household responsibilities, money and finances, social outings, and giving advice. The goal throughout is to use the eating disorder as an opportunity to evaluate what the family needs now, so that each person's individual needs for growth, connection, communication, and privacy are better heard and attended to.

Sharing a Household

When sharing a household with an eating-disordered person, the problems that arise about food and related household chores need solutions that respect everyone's rights but do not encourage or provoke the symptomatic behavior.

Household rules will differ depending on your relationship to the eating-disordered person. If the symptomatic person is your daughter, you are in charge of the household, but her age will determine the number and kinds of rules you establish. In a marriage, one spouse does not make rules for another. There is give-and-take that ideally establishes a comfortable arrangement for both people. For roommates, expenses and household responsibilities are shared jointly by everyone living in the house.

Everyone who lives with an eating-disordered person must face the issue of what kind and how much food to keep in the house. Yet there is enormous confusion about the "right" solution.

Some people we've spoken with keep the house bare of "binge foods"—sweets, pasta, bread, and the like—hoping the bingeing will be curtailed by the absence of such foods. In other households, closets are locked to keep food safe from the binger. Still others keep the house well stocked, hoping the bulimic or binge eater will refrain from "public" binges. And in some households the missing food is simply replaced, and everyone accommodates to the situation as though nothing is amiss.

Rule 3: Don't purchase (or avoid purchasing) food solely to accommodate the eating-disordered person.

Household food is to be shared by everyone. However, binge foods are to be supplied by the person who binges, not by you. Housemates are not to be deprived of foods they enjoy despite the possible temptation to the person struggling with food or weight issues.

When Lawrence and Tanya Morton discovered their 16-year-old daughter, Patricia, was bulimic, Tanya stopped buying any snack food and went from shopping once a week to shopping three times a week so there would never be a big supply of food in the house at one time. This made Lawrence and their two sons furious at Patricia because there was no snack food at home. Besides, they argued, it didn't stop Patricia from bingeing. What it did do was make Patricia feel even worse because now everyone was angry at her.

If your daughter, spouse, or roommate is anorexic, you may be tempted to have food on hand that may entice her to eat or foods you know she used to enjoy. Unless it is at her request or part of a structured treatment plan, do *not* provide food with the purpose of seducing her to eat. It won't work. In the Morton family, all attempts to keep healthy food available for the household failed in changing Patricia's bingeing.

It is crucial that the eating-disordered person not be the focus of the household's food decisions. You may feel as if you are helping her by eliminating all sweets from the house. This is not helpful. What you are doing is preventing her from facing the seriousness of her problem and thwarting her motivation to do something about it. If the rest of the family doesn't want to have sweets around, that is one thing. But this decision should not be made in an attempt to help the person with the eating disorder.

That being said, foods that may be tempting to someone who is struggling with weight issues should not be on obvious display. Get rid of display bowls of Hershey's Kisses, peanuts, or other treats that may be hospitably and decoratively placed in living rooms or dens. They can be dangerous for someone trying to make healthy decisions around food. You don't need to get rid of these tempting snack foods, but do store them out of sight so they are not ongoing challenges to the person struggling with food.

In some households it is helpful to establish food shelves for each household member. Each person chooses his or her own food, and these become nonshared items. If these items are missing or eaten by the eating-disordered person, she is responsible for replacing them. In response to the suggestion that the Mortons have separate food shelves, they devised the following plan:

- Tanya Morton would shop once a week. Common food would be kept in its regular place.
- Five shelves were marked, one for each family member, and the food on that shelf was only for that person.
- Tanya Morton asked each week what everyone wanted for his or her shelf. The Mortons had set a $15 limit on how much would be spent on each person's individual food.
- Everyone agreed not to eat food from anyone else's shelf unless he or she asked permission.

As part of this plan, it was agreed among the family members, including Patricia, that if Patricia ate food from someone else's food shelf, she was required to replace it and forfeit a part of her allowance equivalent to the cost of the food.

Rule 4: If a meal plan has been established by a professional, unless you are
involved in a therapeutic refeeding program with your child, do not
comment on what is eaten.

In these cases, the treatment team or therapist should spell out what
will happen if the meal plan is not followed. Do not encourage the
eating-disordered person to eat, and do not withhold foods from her
because they are fattening or unhealthy. Making someone else's diet
decisions in the home leaves her unprepared for making those decisions outside the home.

Questions like Do you want a taste? and Would it satisfy your craving
just to have one bite? are also not helpful and should be avoided.

Jenny, a 32-year-old binge eater, described what mealtimes had been
like at home:

Mother would always prepare a diet dinner if I were present. I ate those
meals—tuna stuffed in a tomato, no mayonnaise, or plain broiled fish
and carrots—feeling like I was in a hospital. It made me so mad. I'd eat
what I was served, but all the while I was thinking about the cookies I
had stashed in my room.

On the other hand, Maggie, 15 years old and just out of the hospital
for anorexia, spoke of a different kind of struggle:

My nutritionist told me exactly what I had to eat to maintain my weight
gain and stay out of the hospital. I guess I just wasn't ready the first
time around. My mother would prepare exactly what I was supposed to
have on my meal plan, but when I saw the food, something in me just
told me not to eat. My parents were so mad at me. They kept telling me
that eating this meal would keep me from going to the hospital. They
would literally try to spoon feed me. Sometimes they would just lose it

and scream. Once my mother even broke down and cried in front of my brother and sister because I wouldn't eat a potato. It didn't matter. I guess I just wasn't ready. Of course, two weeks later I was back in the hospital.

But the next time around it was different. My parents had a lot more support and somehow were less emotional about the whole thing. They basically said, "It's up to you. If you don't eat, we have to find more residential care for you." I know I made everyone crazy because I kept my weight exactly at the lowest number I could to stay out of another hospital. But somehow this time I knew everyone meant business. I'm not sure if that's what did it, but it's been six months, and so far my weight has been steady. I'm now back at school and spending time with my friends.

Rule 5: Don't make mealtimes a battleground, even if you are refeeding your daughter.

The eating-disordered person should be treated like everyone else and invited to join you at meals if this is how the household generally functions. If she chooses not to come to the table, make it clear that she needs to decide what she is going to do about whatever meal plan or food goals are in place with a therapist, but regardless of what she does with the food, you would like to have her company. Say it in a calm voice, and if she still won't come, say, "Okay, but I hope you'll join us next time." Don't stop asking her to join you, even if she keeps refusing.

If you are in the process of refeeding someone who is anorexic, assume that it may take much longer than the normal family meal for the person to eat. Others may be excused from the table if they can't be part of the support at that point. Be sure that the family meal is not focused only on what the anorexic is eating. Some families have a rule that during the first 15 minutes of the meal, no one is allowed to talk about food (this is often the rule at mealtimes in many residential care facilities). Conversation should be on anything but food. The hard work of sitting with someone who needs help eating bite after bite may be left for later in the meal, after the family has had time just to talk and reconnect.

If your daughter is joining you for the meal, whoever is cooking can tell her what is being prepared and ask if she'll have some. If she says no, she should be free to prepare her own meal (don't do it for her—unless, again, your preparing a separate meal is part of a treatment plan set up with professionals). If desserts have been a part of your family meals, they should not be eliminated. But don't serve any to the eating-disordered person without asking her first. If you know desserts present a problem for her, tell her beforehand you will be serving dessert and that she is free to leave the table before the dessert is served. After all, you wouldn't offer a drink to an alcoholic.

Rule 6: Be willing to negotiate household chores involving food.

No matter how critical someone's eating disorder may be, if she is living at home and not in a hospital, everyone in the family still needs to find a way to manage living with one another. Inevitably, the most mundane situations become loaded with anxiety. Certainly, food shopping and cooking are two of the common household chores that can become highly stressful for everyone involved

There are usually questions about who should do the shopping and cooking. In some households, the eating-disordered person (for example, if she is a spouse or older daughter) may be responsible for cooking or food shopping either all the time or on a rotating basis. If this is uncomfortable for the household member with the eating disorder, consider swapping chores for something that does not involve food.

One mother told us of her 16-year-old bulimic daughter Ellie's attempts to shop for the family food. When Ellie was in a phase of trying to control her eating, the foods she'd bring home would be all low fat, no salt, and sugarless. When she was in a phase of being prone to bingeing, she would bring home substantial amounts of bread, pasta, and chocolate.

The family spoke and decided that her household chore should be changed to doing the laundry. Not being confronted with choosing food every week made Ellie feel better. The family was relieved not to be directly affected by her problems with food.

Rule 7: The eating-disordered person is responsible for her behavior whenever it affects others.

Bathroom Messes

If someone is vomiting, she is responsible for leaving the bathroom clean and usable for the next person. This rule must be inflexible and nonnegotiable.

Darlene Jones agreed with this philosophy. After her daughter Dotty vomited her breakfast, Darlene would insist she clean the toilets, with an eye for detail. Dotty would say, "Yes, Mom," and "Okay, Mom," till she was late for school. Her mother did not want to interfere with Dotty's education and felt that school came first. Since she couldn't bear to leave the bathroom as it was on most mornings, she ended up cleaning it herself.

We were firm when Darlene told us of the morning ritual. Dotty must clean up *before* she goes to school. If she didn't do that and risked being late for school, she would have no computer for that evening except for a designated time to do homework (with no IMs allowed—or the computer would be taken away yet another night). Computer time was a very valuable commodity for Dotty. Two days of uncleaned toilets, and she finally started to change. Her mother continued to feel worried about the fact that Dotty was vomiting, but she had made a significant first step in allowing Dotty to see that the purging was her responsibility and that she had to decide how she was going to handle it.

You are not to take on the eating-disordered person's responsibilities or ease the consequences of her behavior. Such help prevents her from accepting responsibility for herself and growing up.

Replacing Food

If someone binges, she is responsible for leaving the kitchen clean and usable. This includes replacing the food items. If a binge has depleted household or shared supplies of food, these must be replaced in time to be available to others.

If someone feels she has free reign over everyone's food with no consequences, this can be an uncomfortably powerful position. One 17-year-old told her support group she felt as though she were "getting away with murder" in response to her parents' continual replenishment of the food she ate. This was not a position about which she felt pleased.

A plan is necessary for how these situations are to be dealt with.

Developing a Contingency Plan

Rules are useless if you can't enforce them. Along with making rules, you need to have a plan in effect in case they're broken. What you can do about broken rules depends on your relationship to the person and her age. If you are the parent of a child who lives at home and is financially dependent on you, you have more power and different options than if the person is your spouse or roommate.

Carolyn and Neal Simons, parents of an 18-year-old bulimic, Abigail, called us because their daughter continually woke up in the middle of the night and binged on all the available food. The Simons were distraught: On many mornings they opened the refrigerator to nearly empty shelves. They felt they had no control over Abigail and were at a loss about what to do.

We reminded them that they gave her an allowance, bought all her clothes, and had control over her comings and goings. A plan was developed whereby Abigail would pay her parents for the food she binged on from the money she earned babysitting. If she depleted these funds, money was to be deducted from her allowance. If these funds were also used up, she was to be given tasks around the house apart from her usual household responsibilities. Each task was given a monetary value, and she could work off her food debt by doing various chores. Night bingeing is often terribly difficult to stop. The goal wasn't to punish Abigail into becoming binge free. The goal was to have her accept that this was a reality and that she had to take stock of what she was doing. In this case, Abigail got so frustrated that she finally agreed to work with a therapist, something her parents had wanted but had previously felt would be a waste of money because their daughter kept refusing to go.

If the person you are concerned about is a friend or a spouse, negotiate a plan whereby the eating-disordered person is responsible for her behavior.

Sophie and Caron were roommates. Caron's bingeing affected Sophie because Caron ate all the food. They negotiated a plan in which Caron would contribute an additional $50 a month toward the household budget. At first, Caron put off paying Sophie, even though she had agreed to do so. Certainly Sophie could not punish Caron. What she could and did do, however, was to let Caron know she was putting a strain on their friendship. The "consequence," in effect, was the breach that would ultimately occur if Caron would not be responsible in the contract and the relationship. Sophie talked to her, and because Caron valued the friendship, she was no longer reluctant to keep the agreement they made.

In another situation between roommates, where the issue was a dirty bathroom, the eating-disordered roommate agreed to pay for a cleaning person to come in twice a week. She knew that if she didn't keep this contract, she would most likely lose her roommate, and this was not something she wanted to see happen.

A contingency plan is like a business agreement. You establish with the eating-disordered person, in clear and simple terms, what the agreement is. This includes spelling out what the actual consequences of her behavior will be. These are the principles that will help you in developing a contingency plan:

- *Use a contingency plan only in situations where the behavior directly affects you.* Do *not* use it to control eating or purging behavior that does not directly interfere with your day-to-day life.
- *Be sure the consequences are realistic and enforceable.* If you are parents of a minor, a financial penalty is a useful one. If your daughter is too young and doesn't have money, then do what the Simons did and assign a value to different household chores until the penalty is paid.

Another consequence that can be used, if it is realistic, is having the person actually replace the food. In Abigail's case, this was not possible. The Simons lived in the suburbs, and Abigail had no way to get to a store independently.

With a child, the consequence may be in terms of forfeiting something valued, such as computer or TV time. This type of consequence can sometimes be more immediate and therefore effective than a monetary consequence that one might have with someone older.

- *Be consistent.* If you "give in" and don't keep the contract, the effectiveness of all future contracts will be lost. Be prepared to stick to your guns. Expect to be tested. At the outset of a new plan, the person will want to see if you really mean it.

Familiar excuses that you may make to avoid enforcing a contingency plan may be "All right, we'll let it go this time, but the *next* time our agreement holds" or "I would fine you, but I know you have no money." When you hear yourself saying or, better still, thinking these phrases, *stop yourself.* Every time you avoid enforcing a consequence, you are letting the person know that she can avoid consequences and responsibilities.

- *Don't apologize for enforcing your plan.* You were not the one who acted irresponsibly. Expect an angry response to the penalty, and when it comes, ignore it. The Simons were told no matter how much Abigail objected, yelled, or cried, they were to deduct the money from her allowance to replace binge food. We warned them that their daughter might try to wear them down, but that if they held their position, she would eventually learn they meant what they said, and they would learn how to use their authority to everyone's benefit.

- *Don't hold a grudge.* Once you have carried through with your plan and the person has paid for what she's done (in the manner agreed upon), then the episode is over and can be forgotten. Abigail did binge and the Simons deducted the money from her allowance for the missing food, but they continued to be angry at Abigail for bingeing. We reminded them that the contract had to do with Abigail's responsibility for the family food and that that issue was now being handled. This was not a punishment for bingeing.

- *Change the plan as the person changes.* A plan must be flexible so there is a response to the individual's change. For example, if you have made separate shelves in your house so that the individual is responsible for what she eats, then you can negotiate a time limit for that setup. If after a certain period there is no problem with the person's eating food that is not hers, you can discontinue the separate shelves. In situations where a time limit has not been set for the contract and you notice that changes have been maintained, let her know that you've noticed her efforts. Ask her if she'd like to change the contract that has been set up or if she prefers to keep it going for the time being.

Don't Make Excuses for Her

Sometimes eating-disordered behavior can have more dire effects than a messy bathroom or missing food. Loss of a job, loss of friends, or school problems may result from the isolation, self-consciousness, or preoccupation often connected with an eating disorder. Do not provide excuses or help cover up for the eating-disordered person; you will only be prolonging the problem.

Laurie wanted to help when her roommate and good friend, Carla, asked her for a favor. Carla had a particularly bad episode of vomiting that left her with a very swollen face and in a very depressed mood. She did not want to face her colleagues at work feeling and looking the way she did. She asked Laurie to call her boss for her and to tell her boss that she had a terrible cold. Laurie did. Several weeks later Carla asked her to phone in and say she had a bad stomach virus. Feeling unnerved by the whole situation of living with Carla, Laurie attended a support group for family and friends of eating-disordered people. She told the group of her predicament. She was advised strongly and unanimously to stop making it easier for Carla. The longer Carla could run from the various consequences of her problem, the worse it was for her.

"It was a hard lesson," Laurie told us. "I thought lying for Carla was an act of friendship. Now I see that a real friend would not help her hide from the truth. When she asks me, I tell her that because I care about her, I cannot help her that way."

Rule 8: Do not monitor someone else's behavior for her (even if you are invited to) unless this is part of a treatment plan set up with the support of professionals guiding the way.

It is not uncommon, when someone at home has an eating disorder, for family life to revolve around it. A teenager may ask her parents to stay at home in the evenings so she won't be tempted to binge (an activity she will only do in private). In other cases, the parents may prefer not leaving someone vulnerable to the temptations of the kitchen.

In general, decisions about whether you are going out or staying home should be based on how you would like to spend the day or evening. The decision should not be based on being available to control someone's eating.

There are times when bingeing or purging is used by a child or adolescent as a cry for help that doesn't really have to do with the food at all. It may be a way of saying that she needs more attention from her parents. This would be a good issue to discuss in family therapy, where everyone could have a chance to discuss the meaning of the parents' staying home. The parents' decision to spend time with their daughter would then not be based on controlling the binges but would be a way of responding to genuine needs.

In some cases, particularly with young anorexics who are potentially in physical danger, you may decide that your daughter's eating is a main priority and that the entire family is going to do anything they can to help the daughter change. This often is most effective with the support of a professional team. If you have opted to go in this direction, monitoring someone's food is obviously the main focus. The most important issue here is to assess what is working—and what is not. If the monitoring is not resulting in your daughter's moving forward with her health and eating—or if it is tearing the family apart with fights—do not try this alone. Get a professional to assess whether your daughter needs more support—or more independence— in taking hold of the food issues. Even if this kind of program is indeed helping with the food and eating behavior, pay attention to the feelings that get evoked by the intense work involved. In this type of refeeding approach, parents put everything on hold to help their daughter recover. But know that, with this kind of focus, inevitably comes some degree of low-grade (or intense) anger and resentment. If you are involved in a child-focused refeeding program, be sure that there is a place to attend to your own feelings.

In many cases, encouraging an overdependence can be crippling. This does not help the person to develop her own sense of control. Sometimes it may be more respectful and loving to support the person's own attempts to help herself than for you to act as an overseer. A professional can guide you in this regard. For example, if your daughter wants you to keep track of her weight, or report to you what she has eaten, refuse to do these things unless it is a structured part of a treatment plan. If you sense that your daughter is having a hard time with this, continue to encourage her to get more help in support groups or treatment (see Chapter 6 on seeking help).

Questions and Answers on Sharing a Household

The following are common questions regarding household rules.

Q. I found my 15-year-old daughter's laxatives in the bathroom last week. She is in treatment for anorexia nervosa but still uses laxatives to "flatten her stomach" when she eats. I threw them out. Was that the wrong thing to do?

A. Don't go searching through your daughter's private things, such as her purse or drawers. However, if she leaves laxatives or other items, such as diet pills or diuretics, in a noticeable place like a bathroom shelf, then do remove them and comment. It may be a cry for help. Say, "I see you're still taking laxatives. I worry about your health when you do that, and I need to help you find a way to stop." As in all cases of anorexia, your daughter needs medical attention. Be sure the physician and her therapist know about the laxatives. Let your daughter know you are contacting them. (If she were not already in therapy, we would suggest reading Chapter 4, No More Secrets, for advice as to how to proceed.)

Q. My wife was hospitalized for anorexia nervosa. She's been out of the hospital for two months. The other day I noticed she had bought diet foods for the house, and she's eating less at meals. The last time I called her therapist without telling my wife, she got furious at me, but

I'm scared she's going to lose too much weight if I don't do something. What do you suggest?

A. Tell your wife about the changes you've seen in her eating habits. Tell her how scared her behavior makes you feel. Say it is important that she do something about it, and suggest she speak with her therapist. Explain that it is difficult for you to stay out of her eating if she's not talking to her therapist about it. You need reassurance that she is aware she's having a problem. If you are in therapy together, bring this issue up in your couples session. If the changes in her eating persist, tell her you will be contacting her therapist—but make sure she knows you are going to call. Likely the therapist will just listen and won't necessarily comment. Let your wife know that if you don't say anything to the therapist, you will be forced to monitor what she is eating, and you don't want to be in that position.

Q. What about having a rule that our daughter can do whatever she wants outside our house, but in our house no bingeing or purging is allowed?

A. Only make rules you can enforce. Unenforceable rules make you ineffective, and the more of them you establish, the worse the situation will become. Trying to stop your child from bingeing and purging is impossible. Stick with the rules that ensure someone is getting help and that focus on actual behaviors in the house, such as replacing the food from the binge and cleaning up from the purge. Those rules are enforceable.

Q. My husband and I are divorced, and my daughter has been diagnosed as being bulimic. We went to a therapist together, and she told us not to replace food our daughter eats and to make her pay us back if she takes other family members' food. We have joint custody, and when

our daughter is at my house, I can enforce the rule, but my ex-husband is unable to do it. What can I do?

A. Parental agreement, whether parents are divorced or not, is one of the most important factors affecting the recovery of children or teenagers. Developing a united stance is the place to begin. All couples, separated or not, may need some support from a therapist or group in this regard.

Ultimately, you may not be able to do anything to change your partner. In this case, you must establish rules that you will keep in your house, regardless of what your ex-husband does.

When you are in therapy again, let the therapist know what you've observed and your distress about it. The therapist can explore the reasons why your husband might be having a hard time enforcing the rules.

Q. Our daughter is 25 years old and bulimic. She lives with us and binges and purges often. She devours all the food in the house and leaves the bathroom a mess. All our attempts to make her responsible for replacing the food or cleaning up her mess have failed. She refuses to go into therapy. What can we do?

A. Are you financially supporting your daughter in ways other than the living arrangements? If you are, use the financial leverage to insist that she be in therapy if she is going to live at home. Also insist that household rules involving responsibilities are respected. If your daughter is financially independent, discuss the idea that your daughter live elsewhere. As a 25-year-old, she is an adult and can live on her own. If she refuses to accept the rules of your home, you can ask her to leave. This may be hard for you, as you may feel you are abandoning her. By not responding to her negative behavior, however, you are teaching her that she can act any way she wants with no consequences. Tell her you are not helping her get well or become independent by putting up with this behavior. You would be willing to help her by letting her continue to live with you if she were using this support to work on her problem in therapy. Since she is not, you cannot let it go on.

Seek support for you and your husband in couples counseling or in a support group.

Q. We have begun using separate shelves for each person's favorite foods. However, our 15-year-old daughter is constantly buying food that she doesn't eat. If she is going to buy special foods, shouldn't she be responsible for not letting these foods go to waste?

A. Someone with an eating disorder is initially going to feel awkward and confused about making decisions concerning what she'd like to eat. She is going to have to experiment with learning her own tastes, the amount of food she needs, and the types of foods she will enjoy or feel comfortable with. She may need to know that more food is available than she actually wants. Expect that food may very well go to waste at times. (You may put an upper limit on what gets spent.)

Q. What should I say when my wife, who is trying not to binge or eat desserts, asks if she can have a taste of my dessert?

A. Why not? Remember, it is not your responsibility to decide what she should or shouldn't be eating. If you are uncomfortable with this, you might tell her that you feel awkward, given that you know of her wish to avoid sweets. Ask her what she feels would be most helpful for you to say in those instances. Don't feel that you need to know better than she what the best thing to say would be.

Q. I am married to a woman who is bulimic and in treatment for her disorder. When she shops, she doesn't buy desserts because she fears bingeing on them. However, she knows I enjoy these foods, as do our

three children. Isn't it her responsibility to care about our needs, particularly those of our children, as well as her own?

A. Not necessarily. There are times when one of the roles of being a spouse or mother may not be able to be carried on as usual. This is one of them. Sending someone who is eating disordered to buy desserts is not unlike sending an alcoholic to a liquor store. This is a time when you should take over and be the one to buy desserts you and the children like. While you need not be deprived of these foods, it should not be up to someone with a "food problem" to have to choose desserts for the household. Food shopping may not be the best task for her. Switch tasks; you do the food shopping, and let her manage some other household chores.

Q. My girlfriend and I have set up a program that I think might work. She has to tell me every time she binges. She initiated this idea and feels that just the idea of someone else knowing will help her to stop bingeing. It seems to be working. Should I continue doing it?

A. It has been our experience that this is not an arrangement that works on a long-term basis. Initially, having to confess may make the person binge less. But since bingeing and purging are often an attempt to feel in control of a part of one's life, putting someone else in charge eliminates that feeling of control. Then, paradoxically, the only way the person can regain control is to start bingeing and purging again—and there you are, in a control battle with your girlfriend over her eating. There are other ways to show her you care about her. We recommend you back out of hearing her confessions. Say, "I'm sorry, but your eating is up to you. I care about you and wish you would not binge, but I can't stop you and shouldn't be in the position of monitoring you. But if you want, when you feel like bingeing, call me and let me know it's a hard time. I don't want to get into trying to stop a binge, but maybe it would help just knowing I'm there when you are upset."

You might suggest she try working with a therapist or a support group so she has a place to discuss her bingeing.

Money and Finances

If you are in a position of either sharing expenses with or controlling the expenses of someone with an eating disorder, then no doubt the eating disorder has affected decisions or provoked questions about money.

One husband complained to us about taking his wife out to dinner. He felt as though he might as well throw $50 down the toilet instead of paying for food that faced the same fate. The waste of money infuriated him, but he didn't know what to do to change the situation.

A frustrated father wanted to know if he should reduce his 15-year-old son's allowance. The money inevitably went to food, and the father felt as though he were standing by helplessly, watching his son sink deeper and deeper into a pit of overeating.

Parents have asked us whether it would be indulging their daughters' problems by financially contributing to wardrobes of varying sizes. One mother, Juanita Hanes, told us in a family session that she normally enjoyed shopping with Linda, her 17-year-old daughter. At those times they could take off for an afternoon, have lunch together, and talk (and laugh!) casually as they went from store to store. Juanita enjoyed being able to treat Linda to a dress or shirt, and Linda also appreciated the time together. At this point, though, Juanita was reluctant to initiate or even partake in these previously enjoyable moments. Linda's weight fluctuated so rapidly these days that her mother thought it frivolous to spend money on clothes that might be too big or too small in a month or two. Besides, she wasn't sure if she would be encouraging Linda's weight obsessions by buying new clothes. Both Linda and her mother missed the time together, but recently no one had mentioned it—even the thought of shopping aroused too much tension.

Money presents a particular problem in relationships where an eating disorder is present. It is an area in which you may have control that can directly affect the eating-disordered person's behavior. It is a part of the relationship that can easily be abused. And in so many cases the attempts to help the other person can turn into a misuse of this power.

Rule 9: Do not use money to control another person's eating behavior.

Decide what would be appropriate behavior regarding payments, allowances, and shared expenses if the other person weren't eating-disordered. For a child or teenager, give an allowance that is based on her age and related to responsibilities in the house, not determined by the fact that she has an eating disorder. You might talk to parents of classmates to find out what allowances her peers receive.

In the case of the father with an overweight son, the father must decide what he feels is an appropriate amount of money for someone his son's age. If the son decides to spend his allowance on food, that is the son's choice. However, the father needs to be consistent and unyielding toward his son's inevitable requests for more money. This can be tough when the son asks for more money to go to the movies with friends. His father wants him to enjoy himself, but in order for his son to be taught the consequences of his behavior, the father must stand firm.

Juanita Hanes had to decide whether she'd still like to treat Linda to a clothing gift (no matter what the clothing size). Maybe shopping for clothes was just too "heated" now. If so, she and Linda should pick another activity to spend time together. It's important to discuss this frankly and openly.

We know of many families in which the daughters have been offered money for pounds lost. Don't do this! This never works and will only increase your daughter's feelings of failure in the long run. Additionally, it treats her serious eating problem as if it were simply a lack of motivation. This resembles a bribe and usurps the person's own inner commitments to making changes.

There *are* times when money can and should be used as leverage to encourage a child's seeking treatment for her disorder. This was discussed in Chapter 5 and is different from trying to control someone's eating behaviors. When money is considered as leverage, professional guidance should direct your behaviors.

If your spouse has an eating disorder, you will need to negotiate finances as a team and together come up with a plan that is mutually agreeable. The husband's questions about paying for dinners for his bulimic wife should be answered in terms of the couple's mutual understandings and compromises regarding how money is spent in the family, not based on his wife's eating disorder.

Roommates and friends can run into trouble around money as well. Andrea had lent Lynn, her roommate and a binge eater, $500 over the previous year for different weight loss programs. Ordinarily, Andrea would not lend so much money, but she felt her friend was in trouble and needed her help. Lynn's failure to stick to the weight loss programs enraged Andrea, and she told Lynn if she did not lose 20 pounds within the next month, she wanted all her money back.

Unfortunately, it is not uncommon to find people embroiled financially in their friends' food and weight problems. Andrea was advised to make future decisions about whether or not to lend Lynn money in the same way she would decide this for other friends, and that the plan for payback of any loaned funds should be decided in advance.

We helped Lynn and Andrea work out a repayment system for the $500, whereby Lynn made monthly payments over the next 18 months regardless of her success or failure in losing weight.

In general, the overall task is to separate decisions about money from decisions that are made as attempts to govern, monitor, or control someone else's eating behavior.

Questions and Answers Regarding Money and Finances

Q. My daughter is bulimic. She spends all her allowance on food. I won't give her any more money when she asks me for it. I tell her that's all the money she gets, and she has to make choices about what she spends it on. Then she goes to my husband and asks him, and he always gives it to her. What should I do?

A. It is important that you and your husband act as a team. You won't be able to make any effective rules if you don't back each other up. Talk with him about the message he's sending her by giving her more money. Tell him that you know your daughter's health is very important to him, but that he's unwittingly supporting her in her bingeing. You know he doesn't want to do that, and that's why it's important that he not give her any more than her allowance.

Ultimately, if he still doesn't change, you need to stay steady and continue to keep your rules about money clear and predictable. He will have to decide for himself how he wants to deal with his daughter. Your own clarity, despite what your husband does, will still be helpful. Remember, the goal here is not to stop the behavior but to send a message that you expect your daughter to be thoughtful about how she is eating.

Q. Money is missing in our house, and we know our 17-year-old bulimic daughter has been stealing it. My husband and I don't know what to do. We ask her about it, but she keeps denying it, and the money keeps disappearing. What can we do?

A. Stealing is serious business. Contact a family therapist to help you figure out how to proceed because even if you've been mistaken about your daughter's stealing, it is clear there is no base of trust in the family. That, in and of itself, is the cause for concern. In the meantime, as difficult as it may sound, you need to put your money and valuables in a locked safe. Tell your daughter it's very upsetting to you that you don't believe her but that for now you have to protect yourselves. Tell her you want to find a way to trust her again and that the first step is likely going to be to meet with a professional to better understand what has gone wrong.

Q. When our daughter turned 16, we gave her a credit card. Our agreement was that she would ask us before she used the card. For months she had been responsible about using it, but recently she has been charging clothes and not asking us first. Also, we see the bills but never the clothes, so we think she may be selling them at school to get money to buy food. We just recently found out from her that she's bulimic. What should we do?

A. Whether or not your daughter actually is selling the clothes, she still is abusing her credit card privileges. Tell your daughter that the original agreement you had about the credit card still stands. The next time there is a charge on it that you did not approve prior to the card being used, you will suspend her use of the credit card. If you continue to mistrust your daughter, or if she continues to break the rules, a family therapy consultation is recommended.

Q. Our daughter is 26 years old and lives in her own apartment. She earns a good salary but is always asking us for money. We couldn't figure out where the money was going. She wasn't using it for vacations or clothes, and her rent isn't that high. Then we found she is bulimic, and she is using the money to buy food for binges. She's still asking us for money. What should we do?

A. Decide how much money you feel is appropriate to give your daughter each month to supplement her own income. You can let her know how you feel—that you don't want her using the money to support her bingeing. However, you can't stop her from bingeing by controlling the money. The amount you give her should not be based on what she is eating. It is up to her to decide how she is going to use that money. You might want to question, however, whether she really needs your financial help at all right now, regardless of whether she is eating disordered.

Recommend therapy, and if she cannot afford it, then tell her, if it's realistic for you, that the therapy is something you'd be willing to help her with.

Q. Our 16-year-old daughter was picked up for shoplifting food. Should we be responsible for the lawyer's fees?

A. Just giving her the money for the lawyer avoids teaching her the consequences of her behavior. Lend it to her and set up a contract for her to pay you back (at least in part). This arrangement may necessitate her getting a part-time job so she can earn the money. Shoplifting can be a sign of more serious trouble. Use this as an opportunity to talk to your daughter about other concerns she may be having and to question how you may be of some help.

Q. My wife is bulimic and is spending most of our money on food. She does not earn any money herself. Before this started, I would just give her my paycheck, and she would run the household, which included caring for our two young children. Now I feel she's wasting money. How can I stop her from spending the money so freely?

A. Talk to your wife about your concern. Tell her you cannot afford to have her spending that much money on food and that it is depleting the family's resources. For now, since she seems unable to handle the money, you are going to have to take charge of the finances. Decide together what is a reasonable amount to spend for food for a family of four. If it is decided that she can't shop for food right now, then you will need to do that task.

Your wife should still have money that is for her personal use, which you should not interfere with. If she decides to spend that on food, that is her business.

Q. My roommate eats all the food in our apartment. We made separate shelves, and our arrangement was that she wouldn't eat any of my food, but she does it anyway. It's really a burden for me financially. What can I do?

A. Tell her you cannot support her bingeing and that it is interfering in your life. You cannot afford to supply her with food. Arrange that she pay you for missing food. If she doesn't and is generally uncooperative, tell her you will not be able to continue living with her.

Q. My roommate has been borrowing money from me and not paying me back. This is new behavior. I know she has problems with food and is insecure about her weight. I'm worried about hurting her feelings, but I can't afford to lend her money that I don't get back. What should I do?

A. It's important to think about your own feelings in this case. Tell your roommate that you can't afford to lend her money that turns out to be a gift. Tell her you won't lend her any more, and you want her to pay you back what she already owes you. If she doesn't have the money, work out a plan for repayment with her that is agreeable to both of you.

Q. My wife and I both work, so she has her own paycheck. She's bulimic and spends most of it on food. We need her money for our household expenses, so the bingeing is bad for us financially. What can I do?

A. Talk to her about how her bingeing is affecting you financially. Figure out what money you need to run your household and how much each of you needs to contribute from your salaries. When you are each paid, put that amount of money into a joint account. You will need to be in charge of the joint money, but be sure each of you has some separate money so that your wife can contribute to your home but still have control over some of her money. In this way, if she chooses to spend it on food, it will only affect her.

Eating Out, Entertaining, and Food

Going out for lunch, dinner, a drink, or coffee is a natural and pleasant time-honored way to socialize with someone. But when someone has an eating disorder, such normally easy social activities can become fraught with tensions and anxieties for everyone.

When Kathy first told her friends she was bulimic, they were afraid to suggest going out for dinner together. "Suddenly I had 50 offers to go to the movies. You can't talk to someone in the movies." Kathy's friends were walking on eggshells. This is common. After all, you don't want to make matters worse.

Janis's experience was at the other end of the spectrum.

> *Every time a friend suggested having a meal together, I would get panic-stricken. I'd put my friend off by saying no, and I was terrified of eating in public. I would spend the entire week focused on the dinner, what I would do, what would I eat, would I vomit.*

Rule 10: Do not anticipate someone else's needs. Ask!

You cannot know and should not anticipate what will cause discomfort for someone else. For example, clothes shopping can be as anxiety provoking as eating for someone preoccupied with weight. The only way to be sure is to ask. Be willing to negotiate. There are many activities you can share with someone that are not food or weight related. Consider museums, lectures, and long walks.

Try not to take things personally. It is not to hurt you that the person is not eating. When you feel hurt, it means the food problem is escalating to a problem in your relationship (see Chapter 8). Respect that the person is unable to comfortably be in a restaurant situation; this is similar to a recovering alcoholic who does not want to spend time in a bar. When the person feels more in control, she may wish to resume this activity.

Rule 11: Don't make eating out a battle of wills.

This is tricky if you love to eat out and your spouse is uncomfortable eating in restaurants. Talk with her about it. Can she be in a restaurant without eating? Are there certain restaurants that feel "safer" for her than others? Maybe she can read the menu in advance so that she will know what she can eat. Don't worry that this is not "normal" behavior.

If someone is struggling with an eating disorder, it is not realistic to expect that things will be normal. If planning a meal in advance helps the person to feel easier about eating out, that is okay.

You may find you're uncomfortable if your companion is not eating and you are. Don't push her to eat to ease your discomfort, and next time plan to do something else together.

Perhaps you have to entertain for professional reasons, and you need your wife (or husband) to attend. If she is willing to join you at your business dinners, try to appreciate that she is being as cooperative as possible. It is too much to ask her to eat the way you want her to. If her eating habits are disturbing, then don't ask her to accompany you.

If you are a parent, and your child refuses to eat, you may decide not to take her with you when you go out to a restaurant. If you feel you will be uncomfortable, it is better to leave her at home.

Questions and Answers Regarding Eating Out and Entertaining

Q. When we entertain now, my wife won't eat in front of anyone. But after everyone leaves, she eats all the leftovers. She says she's too nervous to eat publicly. I wish she'd just relax and enjoy herself. What should I do?

A. Talk with your wife about whether entertaining is too stressful for her right now. Find out what is harder for her—entertaining at home or in restaurants. It may be that neither situation is comfortable, and you will have to hold back on entertaining with her for now. Talk with her about a plan that will make things easier for her. Tell her it is important to you that you have a social life, but for now maybe you can do things with other people that don't involve eating, such as going to concerts, plays, or movies.

If she decides that she would still like to meet friends over dinner, ask her whether eating at home or in a restaurant will be more comfortable.

Q. My wife is anorexic but not at a dangerous weight. She hates going out to restaurants, but I have to for business purposes. She's agreed to accompany me, but I'm worried because she has strange eating habits that are noticeable to other people, and I'm worried about what my associates will think. What should I do?

A. This is a time when you have a decision to make. You cannot ask your wife to change her eating habits or worries about food. (If she could, she would without your asking her to.) You must decide either to have her accompany you and eat (or not eat) as she wishes, or to attend these dinners alone.

Q. My wife is bulimic and in therapy, but she still won't eat anything at family functions. Both my parents and her parents are asking me what's wrong. I've started making all kinds of excuses for why we can't attend, but I don't think I can keep this up much longer. What should I do?

A. Don't expect her to go to every event. Let her know the ones that mean the most to you, and negotiate which ones she will attend. There may be times that you will have to go without her.

Discuss with your wife whether she wants anyone in the family to know about her bulimia, and if so, whom. If she wants to tell someone, let it be up to her, not you, to discuss the bulimia with that person. Talk together about what you will say to family members when you are asked why she doesn't eat.

Q. My 15-year-old daughter is anorexic. Whenever we go to my mother's house or to a family function, my mother is always on my back about how little my daughter eats. I've been begging my daughter to please eat for my sake so I won't be put in this embarrassing situation. My daughter still won't eat, and it's making things worse between us. What should I do?

A. You need to decide how involved you want your mother to be in your relationship with your daughter. You may want to tell her about your daughter's anorexia. On the other hand, telling your mother may make the situation worse, depending on how helpful your mother is in situations like this. But don't ask your daughter to help negotiate your relationship with your mother. The issue here is really between you and your mother. You have to set limits on your mother's involvement. You can simply and firmly tell her that you don't want her to ask you any more questions about your daughter's eating behavior.

Giving Advice and Opinions

People close to someone with an eating disorder tell us about the quandary they feel when asked for advice and opinions. "How do I look?" "What should I do?" "Am I too fat?" "Am I too thin?" How do you respond to such questions?

Rule 12: Do not offer advice or opinions.

People with eating disorders are often searching for approval from those around them. It is very tempting to reassure them that they look fine or offer your advice about their eating habits, weight, or clothes.

These requests are signs of anxiety and insecurity. Your reassurances or suggestions may at best provide temporary relief. But in the long run they further interfere with the person's ability to develop her own judgment and self-worth.

Be supportive. Tell the person you care and feel badly when she emphasizes her weight and looks to the exclusion of her other qualities and traits.

Rule 13: Do not play therapist.

Be on the lookout to see if you have taken on the role of therapist or professional, thereby minimizing the need for your daughter, wife, or friend to talk to someone on the outside. Do you feel the burden of having to say the "right" thing, ask the "right" questions, listen to unending concerns about eating with the hope of easing the problem? If you notice yourself doing this, step back from taking on these responsibilities, and tell the other person you cannot help her in this way. This will encourage her to look elsewhere for help. Regardless of whether she is in treatment or not, stepping back will also ease the burden you are inevitably feeling and relieve some stress in the relationship. You cannot provide the help you would like to. There is no way for you to be objective or sufficiently detached in this situation. We know that it is difficult to step back. You may feel you are abandoning the person you care about. Be assured this is not the case. When she talks about her troubles with food and/or weight, remind her that you know these preoccupations indicate she is feeling bad about herself. Tell her that there are ways of resolving those feelings and achieving a more positive sense of her self, and, as much as you care, you're not the best person to help her out with these matters. Be sure you let her know that if there are other things on her mind, you would want to talk to her about them and that you are there to support her in other ways.

Rule 14: Do not comment about someone's weight and looks.

Telling someone with an eating disorder that she looks good or thin is not necessarily received as a compliment. Such statements can be understood to mean that looks and weight are being observed and assessed. Even if the comments are complimentary, these remarks can generate a great deal of anxiety about how someone has looked previously and how she will look in the future. While you may give a compliment in an offhand manner or mean it to be supportive, it can have effects far beyond your intent.

Barbara, a 27-year-old binge eater, put it this way:

> I know this sounds overly sensitive on my part, but my boss is always telling me when he thinks I look good. The other day he told me he thought I looked pretty thin—and it got me angry. It made me think that he must have thought I looked fat before that, and then I was annoyed that he's always noticing. I'm worried enough about my weight as it is—I wish he wouldn't make these comments. It makes me feel that if I'm not at a weight he likes, he's quietly criticizing me in his head. I feel like I'm under a microscope.

Questions and Answers Regarding Advice and Opinions

Q. My daughter often asks me, "Am I too fat?" or "Do you think I should lose weight?" She *is* overweight, and I've been telling her to lose weight, but nothing changes, and I'm completely frustrated.

A. Do not feel compelled to answer your daughter's questions. While you may care a great deal about her looks and weight, telling her so is not in her best interests. Chances are she already knows how you feel, and getting you to say so only increases her anxiety and concern regarding a subject about which she is already overly worried. It is important that she determine for herself what her weight should be.

Do tell her that you care about how she feels and that what is most important to you is how *she* feels about her weight. She has to figure out how she wants to look and what is standing in the way of her own goals.

Q. My daughter is bulimic. Both my husband and I are very conscious about our appearance. It does bother us when she gains weight, but we don't want her to control her weight by vomiting. What should we do?

A. Don't make comments to her about how much she weighs. You may be putting a lot of pressure on her. Pay attention to how much you talk about weight and appearance in the family. How important is looking good to you? Sometimes your own family values may make it difficult for you to shift away from a focus on looks and weight. If this is your situation, you may need to do some work on your own emphasis on appearance. It may be harming your child. This work is often best done in therapy.

Q. My husband eats constantly. He was a very heavy child but lost weight before we got engaged. Now he is gaining weight steadily. He asks if I'm still attracted to him. I say yes because I don't think it should be up to me to tell him to lose weight. But I'm not being truthful with him. Should I say anything?

A. Yes. Tell him how you feel about his attractiveness to you. If asked, you might say, "I love you, but I'm more attracted to you when you're in shape." This may seem hard to do and perhaps cruel, but hiding your feelings is worse. Be sure you say it in a gentle, loving way. In the case of a sexual partner, attractiveness is a part of the relationship, and an answer is called for. Note that you would not be advised to respond this way in a parent–child relationship or a friendship.

Q. My daughter, who is overweight and constantly eating, asked me if she should go to Weight Watchers. She also wants me to come with her. She says it will be easier to go together. What should I do?

A. If she wants to go, then you can certainly support that. If she is shy about going alone, you may want to help by joining her for the first meeting, but once she is settled, go your separate ways. If you decide going to Weight Watchers is something you'd like to do for yourself, then go ahead—but to a different meeting. Going together can pull you into her struggles with food. Also, by going, you may be putting yourself in a competitive situation with your daughter, a contest about who loses the most weight or who has the best eating habits. If you do end up attending meetings with her, try not to discuss who is doing "better," and develop other ways to spend time together.

Q. My teenage daughter thinks she's too fat to date, so she refuses any boy who asks her out. I keep trying to tell her she looks fine, but she won't pay any attention to me. What should I do?

A. Her fears and insecurities are beyond the help of a little reassurance. There is nothing you can do to make her date. Tell her you want her to be in therapy or an adolescent support group so she can get some help and not feel so badly about herself.

Q. My roommate, who has bulimia, keeps breaking dates whenever

she feels she is too fat to go out. She's been asking me whether I feel she is inconsiderate when she does this. What should I do?

A. Tell her that while in general she's a thoughtful person, in these situations, she is indeed being inconsiderate. To you, this means that she must be having a hard time. Her conflict about wanting to date and being afraid of it must be terrible. Suggest she join a support group or speak to a professional about the issues troubling her.

8

When It's Hard to Let Go

Understanding What Keeps You So Involved

Each person who reads this book and applies the guidelines set down in Chapter 7 will have a different experience of finding ways to be involved that are helpful. Your experience will vary on a continuum from that of a relatively easy time making the changes we've suggested to finding it almost impossible, regardless of your best efforts and intentions. In all cases, change is a process that occurs over time.

If you find that no matter how hard you try to change, you keep returning to old problems, this is not a sign of weakness or failure on your part. You may feel that you have failed—that is normal. But as in any situation, a challenge is also an opportunity. In this case, if you keep returning to old patterns of behavior, it is an opportunity to question what meaning the involvement has come to serve in your life. Perhaps worrying about the eating-disordered person keeps you from facing even more difficult problems. Perhaps you are relating to the person with the eating disorder the way you have been taught to relate to a parent or sibling in your original family. How deeply involved you are with the eating behaviors will determine how much work you need to do to disengage yourself.

Ginny Stone had been working on being less involved in her daughter Nicky's bouts with bulimia. Nicky, 15 years old, was in treatment and working at resolving her eating difficulties. Ginny, who attended a support group with her husband, wanted to do what was best for Nicky. But she was having a very hard time of it.

> I've stopped asking Nicky what she's eating and if she's vomiting, but I still go into the bathroom after she's left it to see if she's vomited. I find myself lying in bed at night waiting to hear if Nicky is in the kitchen. Lately I've even begun to look through the waste can in her room for candy wrappers or other signs of a binge.
>
> I want to stop, but I can't. I must be somewhat to blame for her eating disorder. She is my kid. I keep wondering if I focused too much on her being thin or if I kept too much food in the house. When Nicky was young, my husband, Michael, and I fought a lot—maybe that did it—making her feel insecure. In any case, I can't get it out of my head that I brought this on somehow. How can I just sit back and not do anything to make her better?

Ginny felt she was to blame for Nicky's behavior. Her guilt and belief that to be less involved with the eating problem was an abandonment of her daughter kept her involved in a way that had consequences for them both. It prevented Nicky from being able to take responsibility for her own behavior. It kept Ginny wrapped up in Nicky's problems to an extent that she could not comfortably put her energy into her own life and marriage.

For Jodie Blauvelt, involvement felt like a life-or-death issue. Her daughter, Maddie, 18, had just been sent home from freshman year at college. She was five feet, seven inches and 98 pounds. When Jodie saw her, she was terrified. Luckily, Maddie was also scared and began to eat a bit more as soon as she arrived home. A physician and treatment team decided that they would begin treatment on an outpatient basis. This was a complicated decision, but Maddie was seemingly now motivated to gain weight and had never had any treatment before, so as a first step, appointments with a therapist, nutritionist, support group, and physician were set in place weekly. The nutritionist, who would be weighing Maddie, set out a meal plan that would allow her to gain about a pound a week.

Jodie, who was raising Maddie on her own, was seen weekly in family therapy in addition to the treatment program set in place. Her role was to provide food for Maddie's meal plan and to support Maddie in her efforts to eat. But she was not to actively comment on what Maddie was eating, nor was she supposed to feed her daughter.

"It was so hard," Jodie reported.

> Maddie would labor over every bite. She was keeping to the program, and she really was gaining weight each week. But at every meal, I watched her like a hawk, ready to pounce if she didn't eat right. I kept making comments to try to get her to eat more or faster. There were so many fights. It just all seemed so slow. She'd take one step forward, then one step back. It was infuriating and almost impossible not to say anything. How do you just sit back and watch your kid die?

Jodie had the most critical justification of all to be involved with what her daughter ate: Maddie could have died. But there were several reasons why Jodie was urged to pull back from the struggles over food. Maddie was an older adolescent whose independence needed to be nurtured, a strong treatment team was in place, and, perhaps most importantly, Maddie was indeed taking steps (albeit small ones) to move forward and take care of herself.

With a tremendous amount of determination and support, Jodie was able to let her daughter struggle to find her own voice regarding her own health and self-care. Maddie did indeed gain the needed weight to return to college—slowly and not without many challenging moments. But what Maddie and Jodie were able to learn from the crisis with anorexia was that Jodie had often done anything she could to keep her daughter from feeling pain. There was always a justification to come in and take care of her daughter. With a situation at hand that Maddie couldn't easily fix, both mother and daughter had the opportunity to witness Maddie's taking hold of her life in a way that hadn't previously happened.

Signs of Overinvolvement

Sometimes your continued involvement will be noticeable to you, as in Ginny Stone's case. For others, the indications are more subtle. The following are signs to be aware of that indicate difficulty disengaging:

- You have difficulty following through with the rules we discussed in Chapter 7; for example, you still cajole, get mad, make comments, and plead.
- Even though you don't want it to, the eating behavior and/or weight fluctuations of your daughter, spouse, or friend can determine how

you feel during the day, making it a "good day" or a "bad day" for *you*.

- You are preoccupied with the eating-disordered person's behavior.
- Your preoccupation results in neglect of other things you should be doing.
- Acting like a detective, you engage in secretive behavior, looking and listening for signs of bingeing, purging, exercising, or the like.

The Justifications

You may feel that your situation is different from others' and that there are good reasons for you to keep on top of the eating disorder. There are always fears, ideas, or rationales that justify an involvement. In Ginny Stone's case, telling herself she was to blame and *should* make it better was the thought that gave momentum to her preoccupation with Nicky. Another woman, Paula, who was married to a binge eater, told us that she could not stop suggesting what her husband should eat because she did not believe he was capable of monitoring his own diet. She was convinced that if she didn't say anything, he'd eat so poorly and get so obese that he would jeopardize his health. "If he dies, it would be my business, wouldn't it?" she asked. "I mean, his dying would certainly affect *my* life!" This rationale kept her embroiled in her husband's eating behavior. The fear was understandable. The problem, however, was that Paula's involvement wasn't making anything any better.

Others stay involved because they feel convinced that the eating-disordered person is doing this to hurt them. "If she cared about me, she would stop," is a phrase we frequently hear.

For example, John told us that his wife, Vicky, knew how much it meant to him that she stop bingeing. If she loved him, she would stop overeating. He could not stop arguing with her about the food because he wanted her to see what she was doing to him.

While every one of these people had their reasons for staying involved, the reasons only masked the more meaningful dilemmas and conflicts in their lives. Ginny Stone was having trouble sorting out her responsibilities as a mother. Was she wedded to some old ideas from her original family? Paula had work to do on why she felt her husband was so incompetent. Was he really? Or was this how she was taught to relate to men? John was measuring Vicky's love for him by what she did or didn't eat. What kept him measuring Vicky's love this way? Was this a holdover from his original family?

Justifications for your involvement may sound good to you on the surface, but they only prolong the eating disorder and keep the areas in the relationship and in your own life that need work obscured from you. We know you are afraid. We know you are trying the best you can. But if your trying is not helping, if indeed things are getting worse, it is time to question how to be involved in another way.

The justifications have the strength that they do because they are fueled by some need you have and probably don't know about to remain invested in the eating disorder. Just as the eating disorder may serve a function for the person with the problem, so too it may be serving a function for you. However, the cost of this to your relationship is high. It keeps you relating to your daughter, spouse, or friend narrowly through her problems with eating and food.

Don't Try to Figure It Out Yourself

The emotional issues that make it hard to change the way you are involved can be multiple and complex. People committed to the treatment of alcoholics have long recognized the need to help the alcoholic's family and friends deal with these issues. Al-Anon was established just for this purpose. The recognition of the need for such support is growing among the eating disorders professional community as well. Often seeking the help of a professional or a support group is the only way to explore and resolve the complicated factors that underlie your entanglement with the food issues.

Your Involvement: What It Means

There are myriad reasons why people stay locked in problematic ways of relating. Each situation is unique. However, in talking with many people about their relationships with eating-disordered people, we have found that there are common factors that seem to influence why people can't change the ways they are trying to help. The following sections of this chapter discuss these factors and examine some of the situations we have seen.

The Effect of Family Rules

As we discussed in Chapter 3, old family rules often make change difficult. In the same way family rules make it difficult for the eating-disordered person to grow up, they may interfere with your being able to find a more helpful way to be involved.

In Ginny Stone's case, these rules were guiding or, more accurately, misguiding her behavior in relation to her daughter. In her family, not jumping in to fix the problem meant you were abandoning your daughter and not fulfilling your job as a parent.

Ronni's and Lilly's situation provides another example of how old family rules operate in current relationships. Ronni and Lilly were college roommates. Ronni spent a year with Lilly, over the course of which Lilly's weight dropped from 115 to 97 pounds. Ronni responded to Lilly in much the same way she had to her father when she was living at home.

In Ronni's family, she had been responsible for her father's feelings. When he came home in a bad mood, it was Ronni, not her mother, who would try to cheer him up. She was the one who would ask about his day and sympathize with him about any problems.

Ronni fell into the same role with Lilly. She would often stay with Lilly instead of going to classes. She thought if she could get Lilly to eat, then all would be okay. She'd buy "goodies" she knew Lilly liked and leave them around the room. In response to Lilly's questions about how she looked, Ronni would try to build her confidence by telling her she looked fine. She didn't say anything about Lilly's increasing exercise regimens.

Ronni's attempts to help were well meaning, but they enabled Lilly to lose more weight undetected. The more fragile Lilly became, the less Ronni asked of her, and still Lilly did not change. Ronni grew resentful, and Lilly became more annoyed as Ronni watched her even more closely.

One afternoon Ronni attended a lecture on eating disorders sponsored by the health services department of the university. It struck her that her situation with Lilly was different from the circumstances at home. While she may have been able to cheer her father up, she realized that all her attempts to help Lilly failed in the face of Lilly's serious illness. She stopped thinking she could change Lilly on her own and suggested they go to the health services department and talk to someone there.

It is necessary that you distinguish between action that is truly helpful and behavior that comes from old family rules and that may prevent someone from taking responsibility for herself.

The Need for a Smoke Screen

Staying involved in ways that don't help is sometimes fueled by a wish to avoid other difficulties that may exist in your life.

Mary James, a 39-year-old mother of a bulimic, shared with her support group the way this happened for her:

> My husband, Marc, and I had a consultation with my daughter Doris's therapist last week. The therapist was concerned because she felt that I was too involved with Doris's eating habits. She asked me what I'd be worrying about if I weren't thinking about Doris. After a long silence and some uncomfortable glances from Marc, I told her that I hated how much my husband drank. I said it so low she didn't even hear me, and I had to say it again. I feel like I can deal with only one thing at a time—and the truth is, I don't want to deal with Marc's drinking. I can't bear to think I'm living with an alcoholic.

As long as Mary was involved in her daughter's problem, she could tell herself that it wasn't the time to confront Marc too. However, both her support group and the therapist disagreed. Mary was encouraged to attend an Al-Anon meeting, and her husband was urged to go to Alcoholics Anonymous. Their therapist told the couple that the issue of drinking could no longer go undiscussed and referred them to a couples counselor.

Substance abuse can be prevalent in the families of people with eating disorders, and frequently a focus on the eating problem hides the drug, alcohol, or other food abuse that may exist among other family members. This cannot be taken lightly. The person with the eating disorder should not have to take care of her problem before other problems are addressed. If you are someone who has worried (even secretly) about your own (or your spouse's) use of food, alcohol, or drugs, it is possible that a focus on someone else's eating disorder might be keeping you from the business *you* need to attend to. Whenever any questions exist regarding drug or alcohol abuse, Alcoholics Anonymous or Narcotics Anonymous meetings (or related organizations, such as Al-Anon) should be attended for information or a source of support, or a professional should be contacted.

Substance abuse, however, is not the only problem that can be obscured by the focus on an eating disorder.

Betty Jo, 20 years old, spoke at a college support group about how her roommate Debbie's eating disorder functioned as a smoke screen for her:

> When everything started happening with Debbie's anorexia, I kind of forgot about my own life. I'd worry about her and be checking all the time for how she was feeling.
>
> It sounds funny now, but it was the calmest I've been in my life. It was good to worry about someone else and not pay attention to myself. Before, I felt so bad and unable to do anything about it. My parents got divorced when I started college, and they'd each call me to tell me how awful the other one was. I didn't know how to stop them. But Debbie's difficulties gave me an unforeseen excuse to change the subject. I noticed that when I'd talk to them about Debbie, they would get worried about her too, and the conversation would focus on her anorexia, not on my parents' mutual complaints about each other.
>
> But once Debbie got into therapy, things changed. She didn't want me to worry about her so much. She made me promise I wouldn't discuss her with my parents. When my parents called, I was back to conversations I had been dreading. One night I spoke to my dorm counselor about it. She suggested I nicely tell my parents that I was happy to talk to them,

but I wouldn't listen to criticisms from one about the other. Then if one of them kept it up, I was to say, "I'm sorry, I won't listen to this. I'm hanging up."

After a few horrible calls, I was able to hang up when one of my parents started getting nasty about the other. After a few hang-ups, they both stopped criticizing the other. I was able to see how angry I was at them for doing this, and I was thankful I got out of it. I even looked forward to talking with them. As long as I had Debbie to worry about, I could shut out my own feelings and put my problems on a back burner.

The Need to Fill a Void

The focus on the eating disorder may make up for something missing in your life. In fact, you may not even be aware that something is lacking.

The void may always have existed, or it may be the result of having focused on someone else to the exclusion of yourself or your other relationships.

Tom was 40 years old when his 13-year-old daughter, Molly, became anorexic. He and his wife, Kathy, 38, spent five years immersed in Molly's problems. They had seen many doctors, followed Molly in and out of hospitals, and struggled their way through five painful years of disrupted meals, emotional battles, and the constant fear that their daughter would die. Now it finally looked like the pain was behind them. Molly was settled in treatment and was maintaining a healthy weight. She was able to leave home for the first time and attend college in another state. Kathy and Tom had just received a spirited letter from their daughter. School was fine, and it looked like she had even started to date. But Tom remained troubled.

I woke up one morning and realized that I was scared to death. Kathy and I had been so involved in Molly's problem that we'd done little else for five years but worry about her. I began to think about how different Kathy and I were—she, so quiet and reserved; me, outgoing, driven, always involved in something. I thought of how rarely we spent time together these days. We were always in separate rooms of the house.

Except for the half hour around dinnertime, when we exchanged information about Molly and her older brother, who was also away at school, we really didn't have much to talk about. I couldn't even remember the last time we made love. I found myself missing the kids terribly. The house was so quiet now. I got scared that I'd be spending the rest of my life in a dead marriage, just waiting for grandchildren so we'd have something to do.

What dawned on Tom that morning was how, in dealing with Molly's problems, both he and Kathy had been ignoring their marriage. Something was missing, and neither he nor Kathy had wanted to face this. As long as the kids were home—and certainly as long as Molly was sick—Tom had no opportunity to feel the deficits in his marriage. But now that Molly was better and just he and Kathy were home, he recognized his long-standing focus on Molly had allowed him to put off the problems he knew were pending in his own life.

Tom and Kathy asked Molly's therapist to recommend a family counselor, and the two of them began treatment. With the help of the therapist, they began to work on rebuilding their marriage together.

The situation of Naomi Kinney and her 18-year-old bulimic daughter is another example of how a void may be filled by attention to the eating-disordered person. Naomi was urged by her support group to leave her daughter Ruth's eating and weight problems to Ruth. She had a very hard time of it. The group suggested she spend more time with her friends and follow through on some of her own independent interests. What soon became apparent was that Naomi did not have any friends, and apart from watching TV and her daughter, she had no interests. Her involvement with Ruth was Naomi's one contact in an otherwise isolated, withdrawn life. At the urging of the group and for the ultimate benefit of both Ruth and Naomi, she went into individual therapy to work on her own fears of people and relationships.

Moving On

It is important to note that no one knows clearly why an eating disorder develops. Every family has its difficulties and challenges. Every family has rules that no longer meet the family's needs. But these situations do not always result in an eating disorder. What we are trying to suggest is not that problems cause eating disorders, but that eating disorders can be an opportunity to address problems—and that when these problems are addressed, there is a better chance that the person with the eating disorder can take hold of her own life and move on.

When we work with someone with an eating disorder, we ask, "If you weren't thinking about food right now, what would you be thinking about?" To the families, we might say, "If you weren't thinking about your daughter's eating disorder, what else would be on your minds?"

If you are involved with someone who has an eating disorder, your experience and role may vary wildly. You may be actively engaged, under the guidance of a professional, in refeeding your child. You may be trying to get someone into treatment. You might be involved with someone who is in treatment, but, nonetheless, you can't stop worrying. No matter what your experience is, this is an opportunity to be curious, both about yourself and about the person with the disordered eating. When a family has a car, the car is usually taken in for a tune-up each year. But when someone has a family, most often, no one takes the family in for a checkup until something breaks down. If you are involved with someone with an eating disorder, this is an opportunity for the kind of fine-tuning that every family needs. What, besides the eating disorder, needs to be cared for? What needs to be communicated? What needs to be changed? The more you understand about your particular family, the more likely you are to set the stage for recovery of the eating disorder. Just as importantly, you are opening the doors for the kind of fine-tuning and change that are necessary in any family to meet the ever-growing needs of everyone involved.

9

Developing a
Healthier Relationship

Relating to the Person,
Not the Eating Disorder

As you begin to stop the kind of involvement that is not helpful, you will be able to gain a clearer perspective on your relationship with the sufferer. It's time to put the past behind you, resolve the frustrations and inequities in the relationship, and reestablish and nurture its strengths.

Improving Communication

An important part of any relationship is being able to talk with one another honestly and comfortably. This takes effort. An equally difficult part of communication is listening without judging and allowing oneself to hear the feelings and dissatisfactions of the other.

Learning to communicate takes practice, especially if your family rules have emphasized that keeping negative feelings to yourself is a virtue or that pretending everything is fine will make things fine.

Katherine and Phil Martin were having difficulties with their daughter, Kelly, who was 16 years old and bulimic.

Katherine told us:

> In our family, we lived by the old adage "If you don't have something nice to say, don't say anything." When Kelly turned 14, she started disagreeing with us about all sorts of things. She raised her voice all the time. This infuriated both of us, but we didn't know how to respond, so we ignored it. Her rage escalated to where she called us names, slammed doors, and broke plates when she was really angry. We tried not to pay attention because of the eating disorder. We didn't want to make things worse.
>
> Phil and I finally went to see a therapist because we just couldn't handle the situation. The therapist encouraged us to regain our right to be respected as parents, but she also pointed out that Kelly had the right to express feelings. Slamming doors and vile language were not considered "expressing feelings." Kelly needed to talk about the differences she had with us without acting like a possessed demon. We in turn had to learn how to listen to her complaints.
>
> The therapist suggested we have family meetings once a week when we could talk together. If someone didn't like a house rule or how someone was being treated, this was the time to bring it up. We told Kelly she could tell us about her anger, but she could not call us names or break dishes. And tell us she did! She had a slew of complaints, some reasonable, some not so reasonable. The tough part for Phil and me was listening to it all and taking Kelly's complaints seriously. We've had to sift through them, and actually Kelly has become more reasonable over time. I guess she was like a pressure cooker, holding all that back and then exploding.

Matthew, 34, discussed his difficulties communicating with Monica, his 32-year-old wife and a binge eater:

Whenever she's upset, she cries and then goes and eats—she never gets mad and really tells me what's disturbing her. It's like a guessing game. I find myself walking on eggshells with her.

There were many reasons why this couple had trouble talking with one another, but they had nothing to do with Monica's eating habits. While Matthew invited Monica to tell him what was bothering her, in fact he would get angry in response to her criticisms. And Monica held back for fear of being too much of a burden to him. She worried he'd leave her if she complained too much.

To start them off, their therapist suggested that they set aside a half hour a week, after the children were asleep, to talk. Monica was to have the floor for 10 minutes only, and then it was Matthew's turn. Monica was to tell her husband all her gripes without interruption. Matthew's job was to listen, and he could not interrupt. Then for the following 10 minutes, Matthew was to talk about how he felt about what was said. If he was upset, this was the time to say it, not while Monica had the floor. The last 10 minutes was to be spent negotiating a plan that would take into consideration both their positions. If the discussion felt too heated for them to come to a negotiating position, then Monica and Matthew would set aside a specific time in the next three days to discuss the issue again, using the same formula. This could be done as often as it took for both Monica and Matthew to feel satisfied with the results. Then it would be Matthew's turn to speak and Monica's to react. As their communication got better, they could increase the time limits.

"It was an eye-opener," said Matthew.

I had no idea Monica was so unhappy about so many things and that I could be so defensive. I thought I was a good listener, but I really wasn't. I thought the only problem was that Monica couldn't be open with me. But I found out that there was another side to this problem—I had a hard time listening. She still has her problems with bingeing, but they don't upset me as much. What matters to me is that we're talking a whole lot more.

Learning to communicate entails both learning to express yourself and learning to listen effectively. Don't let your emotions get in the way of your ability to listen. And remember, focusing on the eating disorder can interfere with both communicating and listening.

Guidelines

Here are some general guidelines to keep in mind for improving communication:

- Do not assume someone else's intentions, thoughts, or feelings.
- Do not blame or attack the other person.
- Do not say "you always" or "you never."
- Do not bring up every issue in your relationship that you are upset about. Stick to the one problem you are discussing.
- Do not induce guilt. For example, "You're killing me when you do . . ."
- Speak with "I" statements. (See Chapter 4 for a more detailed explanation.)
- Balance your communication: be sure people know what you like as well as what you're unhappy with. Be generous with praise, but only if it's sincere.
- If need be, establish household meetings to pave the way for open

communication. Establish ground rules that allow people to speak freely without fear of an angry response or retaliation.

- Listen with an open mind, not a defensive one.
- Be willing to seriously consider others' gripes and to work toward a mutually satisfying agreement. Notice when you are not really taking the other person's concerns seriously, and try to imagine how you would respond differently if you really accepted what was being said.

Establishing Responsibilities

In any marriage, intimate relationship, or household, responsibilities are divided. Sometimes what develops works well and feels fair; other times it doesn't.

As we discussed in Chapter 3, in families in which there is an eating-disordered child, there may be imbalances in the area of establishing responsibilities in the household. Many times parents err in one direction or the other, taking over too many tasks for the children or burdening them with responsibilities beyond their capacities. To make matters more complicated, both situations can exist at the same time. For example, a bulimic teenager may be left on her own scholastically (even if she is doing poorly in school), while at the same time her parents insist on early and nonnegotiable curfews.

In evaluating the responsibilities your eating-disordered child has, you must realistically consider her age and her capabilities. Do not work around her eating disorder, viewing it as a handicap; this will only discourage her from feeling competent. Helping someone grow up includes allowing her increasing rights and responsibilities regarding decisions about her own life (that is, what to wear, what friends to have, what activities she can participate in).

Roger Cohn and his wife, Patty, grappled with this situation with Cynthia, their 16-year-old daughter, before they were seen in family treatment. Cynthia fluctuated between bulimic and anorexic-like behaviors. Roger spoke of their situation this way:

> It was hard for us to think of her as being 16. She always seemed and acted younger. She'd ask for our help with almost everything, and we were pleased to support her. But it seemed we were doing the same things for her at 16 that we did when she was 4. We knew if we didn't help, we'd be in for a fight, and it just didn't seem worth it. Cynthia didn't even clean her own room—we did. Every morning my wife would make Cynthia's bed and pick up all the clothing off the floor.
>
> When we began therapy, we had to reevaluate things. The therapist told us that Patty and I had to help Cynthia grow up.
>
> The first rule we established was that Cynthia's room was her responsibility. She could keep it as neat or as messy as she wanted. If she wanted clothes washed, she'd have to make sure they were in the laundry bag. We didn't want to see the mess in her room, so we asked her to close her bedroom door when she wasn't home. Cynthia would provoke us sometimes by not closing her door. My wife and I are very neat, so it wasn't easy to leave her room alone. We insisted that the rest of the house be kept clean. This was common property, and Cynthia had to pitch in.
>
> For the first time, we gave Cynthia an allowance. Before this, whenever she asked for money for anything, we either gave it to her or not, depending on whether we agreed on how she wanted to spend the money. Now she was given $25 a week to spend as she pleased. In exchange for her allowance, she was expected to take out the trash, walk the dog, and help with the dishes each night.
>
> Then we worked out a system to handle Cynthia when she left things

around the house. She would be asked twice to pick up after herself. If we had to ask a third time, we subtracted $1 from her allowance for every item left around the house. We didn't scream. We didn't yell. We just deducted money from her allowance.

We've been doing this for three months, and now that the rules are clearer, Cynthia has become more responsible. We spend much less time arguing and much more time talking with her about other things in her life, like school and friends. I think Patty and I were sort of surprised too that someone who had as many problems as Cynthia did—starving, bingeing, fasting—could actually be responsible. It's been nice to be able to see our daughter in this new light.

By giving Cynthia more responsibilities, the Cohns were telling her that they felt she was capable of taking care of herself, an important message to support her sense of competency. They were also respecting her as a person with needs, values, and preferences that were different from their own.

In marriages or friendships in which one person is eating disordered, responsibilities may not be fairly divided. When that happens, the balance of responsibilities must be renegotiated between the people involved.

Mark, the 30-year-old husband of Justine, 28, talked about the division of responsibilities in their marriage:

In our relationship, I tended to be the one in control. I like to be the one in charge, and Justine went along with that because she felt taken care of. It never occurred to me that she was unhappy. Until Justine became anorexic, things were going fine.

But when Justine stopped eating, I went nuts. It was the first time in our marriage I wasn't in control. Nothing I did could make her eat. In the support group she began attending, she was encouraged to make more decisions in our relationship. Now she tells me we have to renegotiate our marriage so it's equal between us, and I'm not making all the decisions. I'm not sure whether Justine can make decisions for herself, let alone for the two of us. How is she going to tell me what to do if she can't even figure out what she should eat?

Mark and Justine had a marriage that was based on Mark's need to have someone to take care of and Justine's desire to be taken care of. Ironically, Justine's anorexia was her attempt at doing things *her* way, and yet it also proved to Mark that she was incompetent and needed his help. However, when Mark attended a family support group with Justine, the men in the group urged him not to just see Justine as sick. It was important that Justine learn to take charge even if she was anorexic.

Now Justine and Mark have to renegotiate a marriage based on equality. If they succeed, they will have a chance at a relationship that is enjoyable and pleasurable to them both. In order for change to occur in any relationship, you must be willing to evaluate and balance how decisions are made and how responsibilities are shared. If both parties are not willing to make this change, the marriage will most likely end or remain chronically troubled.

Guidelines

Here are some guidelines for improving the balance of responsibilities in your relationship:

- If you are parents, look at the rules your family has regarding responsibilities. When children or teenagers are involved, you must make sure the responsibilities are appropriate to their age. If you're not sure, consult with friends, teachers, or support groups to find out what responsibilities are typical in your community among children of the same age.

- If there is disagreement between parents and children, parents ultimately set the rules—but not without hearing their child's opinions. When in doubt, speak with other parents or professionals to establish reasonable expectations of your child.

- Between adults, be sure the division of responsibilities is fair and appropriate for everyone involved. Each person's responsibilities should be clearly spelled out so nothing is assumed or taken for granted. Do not minimize responsibilities if someone is eating disordered.

- If there are areas of disagreement, either a household meeting or a planned time to talk can provide a forum for discussion. Use the guidelines suggested for communication when you hold these meetings.

- Among adults, disagreements with regard to responsibilities should be negotiated openly until a fair arrangement is agreed upon. When difficulties seem insurmountable, a support group or professional advice can provide helpful guidance.

Respecting Rights

Imbalances that exist regarding responsibilities inherently create imbalances regarding people's rights. This may include the right to age-appropriate freedoms, to privacy, and, when a child is involved, to be taken care of.

As we discussed in Chapter 3, a focus on an eating problem can obscure these rights.

The Right to Grow Up

One problem we commonly see is that when children with eating disorders mature, they are prevented from experiencing the freedoms they should be granted as they get older. In our earlier example, we discussed how Cynthia Cohn was not expected to assume responsibilities typical of a 16-year-old. This was not the only way in which she wasn't treated her age. Her father was nervous about her going out on dates or even hanging around with her girlfriends in the evenings. As a result, Cynthia had to be in by 10:00 p.m. on weekends. By her parents' standards, this was a fine compromise, but Cynthia ended up feeling like a baby among her friends, all of whom had much later curfews.

Part of the work in the Cohn family was not only considering responsibilities, but reevaluating the rights and freedoms of family members. Having a 10:00 p.m. weekend curfew was unreasonable for a trustworthy 16-year-old in the community where the Cohns lived. The Cohns were urged to speak with other parents of 16-year-olds to find out what curfews they had for their teenagers. After doing this, a 12:00 a.m. curfew was finally decided upon for the weekends, with the compromise that Cynthia would keep her parents informed as to where she was spending her time, and that there were some nights she could plan to sleep at a friend's house and abide by that family's rules (there was a 12:30 a.m. curfew in that family).

If Cynthia did not respect the curfew and rules, if she did not call or was more than 15 minutes late, she was grounded one night the next weekend. This was not negotiable. Cynthia could complain, but the agreement would stick. No matter how important the week's missed event might be, if Cynthia was late, she had to pay the consequences.

The Cohns were urged not to evaluate Cynthia's rights based on her eating behavior. She was 16 years old, regardless of how or what she ate, and she needed to experience the freedoms that other adolescents her age enjoyed. Her trustworthiness would be based on how she handled these freedoms, *not* on how well she recovered from an eating disorder.

The Right to Be Taken Care Of

Rights have to do not only with letting a child grow up and become independent, but also with protecting her from having to grow up prematurely. A child or teenager has a right to be able to depend on her parents to be there as sources of authority, security, and comfort—without having to ask.

In Rayann's situation, she and her mother were very close. Her mother, Susan, was very caring and worked hard to provide a good upbringing for her only daughter. Rayann's parents had divorced when she was three, and neither she nor her mother had seen her father since. Rayann was now 14. Susan felt that she had done the best job she could as a single mother. Rayann had been healthy as a child, did well in school, and was very involved socially with a group of friends whom Susan liked and respected. Only Rayann's bulimia was a clue that something might be wrong. When Rayann went into treatment for her eating disorder, Susan joined a mothers' group because she wanted to know what to do to help. Susan describes the outcome of the meetings this way:

> *Rayann and I always have been close. She can talk to me when something's on her mind, and I am able to talk to her whenever I'm upset. I always thought this was a good thing, but in the group I learned that maybe I had become more of a friend than a parent.*
>
> *The group helped me notice how much I depended on Rayann to be*

there for me. I never thought this was bad, but the group felt that it was encouraging Rayann to be responsible for me. There were certain things they said I shouldn't be talking to her about, like how I felt about men and sex, how lonely I was, how much her father had let me down. Not that I should be phony, they told me, but just that these were adult issues and could feel burdensome to a teenager. What was apparent was that Rayann had become my closest friend and that as long as I relied on her in this way, she would feel burdened.

Susan was urged to stay in the group in order to develop a support network beyond her daughter. The group helped Susan refrain from certain discussions she normally had with Rayann—in particular, regarding sex, men, Rayann's dad, and her loneliness. As Susan was able to depend on her peers instead of Rayann, she noticed a burden was lifting from her own shoulders. While she had enjoyed her closeness with her daughter, she also had often felt shaky—after all, relying on a 14-year-old is not a secure position for an adult to be in. With a newfound source of support (the group) and newly felt experiences of security, Susan noticed that she was enjoying her daughter in a different way. She didn't expect as much from Rayann anymore. And she noticed that Rayann seemed to feel relieved; in fact, it seemed she was turning to her mother more these days with her own questions about guys, school, and clothing. For the first time, Susan felt confident about being a mother, not a peer, to her 14-year-old.

Because Susan sought help in response to Rayann's bulimia instead of just trying to change the eating disorder, she was able to work on the areas in her relationship with her daughter in which she could affect change and be of help.

Because children like Rayann are so quick to fill in and do the jobs asked of them, it is easy to miss how deprived these children feel inside. While they may be very needed and important to their parents, they can also be suffering from neglect, a neglect no one sees. Often it is easy to miss how in need these teenagers are of parents' time and comfort. When this is the case, their rights as children or adolescents are being overlooked.

In another example, Henry Phillips spoke about the relationship he and his wife, Connie, had with Elana, their 13-year-old bulimic daughter:

> *Connie and I are both professionals. I'm a screenwriter, and Connie is an internist. We work long hours and love our careers.*
>
> *Connie leaves the house early in the morning to make hospital rounds and has office hours until 7:00 p.m. When we eat together, it's around 9:00 or 10:00 p.m., and Elana has long since finished. When I am home, I'm often writing.*
>
> *We've always relied on a live-in housekeeper to keep things running smoothly. Our older son, Jeremy, 17, never had any problems. He does well in school, has lots of friends, and the girls are crazy about him.*
>
> *Everything seemed fine until Elana became bulimic. This stopped us in our tracks. We made sure she saw a therapist right away.*
>
> *Elana's therapist wanted to see all of us, but we couldn't find a time that all four of us could make. I'll never forget this scene: Connie was on the phone with the therapist, and we were looking at our schedules. Elana was sitting on the couch near the phone and could hear the conversation. The therapist would mention different times, and either Connie or I would say, "No, that's not a good time for me." After a few minutes of this, I noticed Elana was crying.*
>
> *The therapist must have sensed what was going on, and she said,*

"Your daughter is in serious trouble, and you need to make this a prior-
ity, or things will get worse. Here are the times I can see you. See which
will work best for you, and call me back tonight."

When Connie got off the phone, Elana screamed, "You have time for
everyone but me." We realized we had better reorganize our lives, or
Elana would suffer.

In the Phillips family, Connie and Henry valued their own independence and encouraged this quality in their children. They tried to be
responsible parents, and when they arranged for treatment for Elana,
they felt they were handling the situation as best they could. But therapy could not do it all. Other aspects of their relationship with Elana
needed attention—they needed to be more available as parents.

In family sessions with the Phillips, this issue was the main focus of
their work. Connie and Henry had to arrange their schedules so they
were available to spend more time together as a family. Family dinners
were encouraged. Elana needed and responded well to having the security and closeness of being with her parents.

The Right to Privacy

In the Phillips family, the parents' needs for their independence and
private lives interfered with their daughter's need to be taken care of.
However, it is important that you not create an imbalance in the opposite direction. In any household or relationship, everyone has a right to
some privacy.

In some families or households, time alone may be seen as an insult
to other household members or a signal that something is wrong, as
opposed to a natural developmental or personal need. If in your family
love is measured by involvement and time spent together, you may have

trouble establishing privacy for yourself or allowing it for others.

"I remember the first time we decided to shut our bedroom doors at night," said Marlene, a school administrator in her forties:

> We had been leaving them open since our girls were babies, and somehow it never changed. Now our daughters are 14 and 16. Our oldest, Lydia, protested all along about this open-door policy, but we found it hard to make the change. Somehow it seemed safer to us to leave the doors open. Our support group, however, had a different view and felt strongly that Lydia needed her privacy. After years of being anorexic, she was actively struggling to feel more grown up, and the group felt we needed to support that. At first, I felt that it was unsafe to have Lydia close her door. She was so skinny—what if something happened to her during the night? If she got up and fell, I wouldn't hear it. Her doctor had told me this was ridiculous, but I still worried. The group insisted that I treat her according to her age, not according to my fears.
>
> We decided to try it. That first night I lay in bed listening to the silence of the house. Oddly, my children felt so far away from me. My husband's steady breathing only made me feel more alone. I thought how crazy this was, that just a shut door could make me feel this way. I think it's the first time I realized that maybe I was having a hard time letting them be on their own.

The mere act of closing doors in and of itself is an important stand in allowing for privacy in relationships.

Marlene was willing to make changes in her behavior, to shut doors and to be honest with herself about her own difficulties. Marlene's soul searching led her to a willingness to respect Lydia's need for independence.

The eating-disordered person is not the only one who needs privacy.

Every individual has that right, including parents.

Peggy, a 42-year-old stockbroker, talked about trying to work during her 18-year-old daughter Jane's struggle with bulimia:

It seemed as though every time I turned around, Jane was calling me. Sometimes she'd call 10 times a day. I felt so guilty if I didn't talk to her, but my stomach would tighten, and I could feel my anger as soon as I heard her voice on the other end of the line. The phone calls were upsetting. Even after the call was over, I'd have a hard time concentrating on my work. Finally, my boss told me I couldn't do both things. It was impossible to do my job and speak to her that often. I decided to call Jane's therapist to see what to do. Jane was mad, but the therapist suggested that I attend a session and that we all brainstorm how to handle Jane's calls. We came up with the following plan:

I set aside time every day when I would talk to Jane outside of work. She lives with me, so we could easily arrange time when I wasn't working. I told Jane that if she wanted to talk to me, we could have breakfast together every morning at 7:30. I didn't care whether she ate, but I wanted her to sit with me.

During that time she could talk about anything that was bothering her. Then she could call me once during my lunch hour between 12:00 and 12:15 p.m. and once after the market closed. In the evenings I'm home. If Jane was home and wanted to speak to me, we could talk then.

If Jane called me at any other time, I was to say I'd speak to her at our next arranged time and then hang up. I was to do that no matter how many times she called. This way, I was available to her but not controlled by her. Her therapist suggested that during these times, she could write down her feelings and speak to me about them later. Or she could bring them into the sessions to discuss there. Then Jane wouldn't feel that she was just being dismissed.

We all tried these things out. The first two days were miserable. Jane didn't wake up for breakfast, she never called me during the arranged times, and she certainly didn't write anything down. Instead she would call at other times. However, after two days of my insisting she call at the arranged times, she slowly started following the schedule. It's now been three weeks, and she occasionally calls when she's not supposed to, but I keep to the schedule. There are days now that she doesn't even call at all.

Now that this schedule is working out, I still worry, but I'm not walking around angry at Jane all the time. We seem to be enjoying our time together more. She asks me to do more things with her, like go shopping or to a movie. I spend my time at work without feeling guilty, and we're much less frustrated with one another.

It is not only individuals who need privacy in a relationship. Parents, as a couple, need to be able to establish private time for themselves apart from their children. Without this, both the parents and the child can suffer.

This had been so for many years with the Kasins. Lynn and Eric Kasin, both 43, had been seen for couples therapy as part of the treatment plan for their 15-year-old bulimic daughter, Alicia. At the time the Kasins entered therapy, Alicia was binge vomiting four or five times daily, or she would eat nothing for days at a time.

One of the striking aspects of Lynn and Eric's relationship was how little time they actually spent with one another apart from the children. Eric, a contractor, tended to work late, and when he was home, he and Lynn spent most of their time with Alicia.

Lynn and Eric's therapist noted how guilty they felt about spending time away from their daughter. How could they have a good time when she was suffering? The therapist reminded Lynn and Eric that it was not helping the situation for them to focus on their daughter and her problem to the exclusion of their own lives. Lynn and Eric's "rule" about how to be good, caring, close parents was actually preventing Alicia from growing up and keeping them from enjoying their marriage. The therapist suggested that Lynn and Eric go away for the weekend.

At first, the Kasins were enthusiastic about this idea and appreciated the "permission" to go off on their own. They arranged for Eric's mother to take care of Alicia and their two younger children, and they spent a couple of weeks eagerly planning a romantic weekend away.

When the weekend arrived, two hours before they were scheduled to leave, Alicia started to cry and said she didn't want them to go. She threatened not to eat the whole weekend if she had to stay with her grandmother. She had become accustomed to being the center of her parents' activities.

Fortunately, Eric and Lynn's therapist had predicted this might happen. Alicia was not used to being away from her parents, and consequently feared being without them and on her own. In the past, her parents would not have gone, causing Alicia to believe she could *not* be on her own. This time was different.

Eric and Lynn turned to the plan they had formulated in therapy about what they would do if this happened.

First, they both told Alicia they were still going away.

Second, they said they were sorry she was so upset and that she wasn't going to eat. If on Monday, when they came back, she still wasn't eating and they thought she was in physical danger, they would contact her therapist, who would evaluate whether the situation was critical enough for her to need hospitalization.

They then told Eric's mother to make meals the way she normally would and to set a place for Alicia. If Alicia refused to eat, her grand-mother shouldn't push it or get into any fights with her. Eric and Lynn would handle the situation when they came home.

Last, Eric and Lynn explained that they would call once a day to hear how things were going.

Eric spoke about the weekend:

> It was rough getting out of the house. Alicia was crying, and my poor mother was almost as upset as Alicia. Our two younger kids tried to pretend nothing was happening. We were determined, though. We hadn't been away alone since Alicia was born, and we were set on getting the time now.
>
> We had picked this beautiful country inn, and it was early spring, so the weather was lovely. We worried about Alicia during most of the ride but vowed not to talk about it. As soon as we got to the inn, we felt better. We decided to eat dinner before we called home. It was delicious, and we had a great bottle of wine. When we called home, Alicia had not eaten and refused to come to the phone to talk to us. Saturday we slept late, had a big breakfast, took a long walk, and went shopping. Then we came back to the inn and made love without worrying about interruptions. It was terrific.
>
> That day when we called home, Alicia had eaten dinner but still wouldn't talk to us on the telephone. What was new for us was that even though she hadn't eaten on Friday, our Saturday hadn't been spoiled. We were getting along, we had a plan for what to do if Alicia didn't eat, and neither one of us let it ruin our weekend.

For Eric and Lynn, their marriage had been subsumed by their worry about Alicia, and they had forgotten the pleasure they could get from each other.

Guidelines

Here are some guidelines to help you ensure that everyone's rights are being respected in your relationship:

- If you are parents establishing ground rules for your children, freedoms should be commensurate with age. Check with other parents in your area to see what curfew times are considered reasonable, how much allowance is considered fair, and what other rights and freedoms are granted.

- A child should not be treated as a friend or as someone beyond her chronological years. Do not tell your child your marital or sexual problems. If you are doing so, you must STOP. If you have questions in this regard, a peer support group is an excellent way to get help establishing appropriate areas of discussion with your children.

- Children have different needs in terms of their parents' time. If your child or teenager is complaining that she does not have enough time with you, listen carefully. She may be right. This may be a point in her life when she needs to spend more time with you. If this is the case, plan the time to be with her.

- Individuals in a household have a right to private time and to closed doors.

- Establish clearly what times or areas are off limits to others' calls or visits—and also establish times when you *will* be available. For example, while work is off limits, you might want to make it clear that you will be home for dinners or available to talk during your lunch hour.

- Couples need time alone without children, friends, or relatives. If you find that you and your spouse do not spend enough time alone, set

up a plan to have dinner or to go out by yourselves. If you have difficulty doing so, the guidance of a peer group or a professional can help
you arrange a plan suitable for you.

Strengthening Your Relationships with the Eating-Disordered Person: Having Fun

And finally, don't forget to laugh.

The most effective way of strengthening a relationship with someone
is to be able to have fun together. When there is a crisis in a family
or relationship, certainly when someone has an eating disorder, this is
often the first thing to go. But trouble involving the eating disorder is
only one aspect of your relationship. There are still many ways to share
interests, feelings, thoughts, and pleasures. Don't forget the many other
ways you can enjoy each other and continue to have fun.

"Things were different before my husband and I got married," said
Georgette, 33, about Kevin, 38 and a binge eater:

> *Everyone loved being with Kevin, especially me. But once we got married,
> it seemed like I forgot some of that. He would get me so angry because he
> was always eating or thinking about food. I was really worried about how
> much junk he'd eat, and we started to argue about that all the time.*
>
> *Things got bad between us. We finally saw a couples therapist. The
> therapist encouraged me to recall some of the things I had loved about
> Kevin. He has a great sense of humor and likes to do fun things like
> going to zoos, amusement parks, the racetrack, all kinds of stuff. So the
> therapist suggested that we do those things again and asked Kevin to
> pick something that was a little crazy, a little offbeat, like the things he
> used to suggest.*

I, in turn, made a vow to shut my mouth about the eating and just enjoy what we planned to do.

It wasn't so easy getting off the food police squad. I started to notice how much I worry all the time. But last month what really hit me was how I'd stopped letting myself enjoy Kevin. We were at an amusement park with my nephews, and I could see Kevin was really enjoying himself with the kids. He was so easy and filled with laughter. And me—I was worried about whether he was going to eat hot dogs and cotton candy.

It was as if for the first time I finally understood how involved I was with Kevin's eating. Here, everyone else, including Kevin, was having a good time, being silly, having fun. And all I could do was worry. Every time I start to worry about Kevin, I think of that day in the amusement park, and I'm able to stop—at least for a moment.

Last weekend Kevin told me that he noticed I haven't been on his back lately, and he thanked me. I can't believe how close I've been feeling to him these days—I wasn't sure that feeling would ever come back. I guess it helped to see that I'm not all that easy to be with too.

When Chrissie Small became anorexic at 13, it seemed that the whole family fell apart. Three years later, Maggie, her mother, described how things began to turn around:

For three years, things have been so tumultuous. Our lives revolved around Chrissie, especially when she had to go into the hospital. All our conversations centered on trying to get our daughter to eat. These last few years have felt like a blur—I don't seem to remember anything else except problems.

It's funny, about six months ago, Chrissie got out of the hospital and began to eat normally, but our lives didn't change much. We still mostly talked about Chrissie's anorexia and her progress.

A month later, though, Chrissie got a part in the musical Grease, in her high school drama class. She asked us for help in learning her lines, and we spent part of our evenings doing that. Even our 16-year-old son, Jed, got involved. I was sitting there one night, and it hit me that we were laughing as a family. I'd forgotten that sound. I'd forgotten that Chrissie had talents. During the time she was anorexic, that was all she was to me—a starving daughter whom I was trying to save.

We had so much fun helping Chrissie with that musical that when our church planned to put on a play for a fund-raiser, all of us tried out and got parts. We were having fun again, and it felt good.

There is only one basic guideline to regaining fun in your relationship and that is

- It is okay to enjoy each other whether an eating disorder exists or not.

Enjoying one another may involve pursuing a project or activity that everyone likes. It may entail setting aside time to be alone with one another or to join other friends or members of the family in activities that were fun prior to the development of the eating disorder. While you can make an atmosphere more conducive to having fun, while you can plan the time or activity, enjoyment is something that you can't make happen. It is a natural process that occurs between people when no obstacles are put in its way. A focus on the eating disorder can become an obstacle. Notice if this is the case in your relationship and work on removing it.

On the Road to Recovery: Both Hers and Yours

Someone with an eating disorder has a long road to recovery. How she manages food and weight issues along the way will be part of her independent struggle to get well. What you do can make a big difference, both for you and for her. Remember, this is an opportunity to fine-tune your relationship and to provide a strong base from which everyone can grow and change.

You may be in a treatment program that encourages active intervention with the eating problems, or you may have been urged to get disentangled with the food battles. Regardless of the position you are taking, there is much to do to help that doesn't just involve food and weight.

There are ways in which you can create an environment that allows for a richer, fuller way of relating and that can minimize the need for the maintenance of a symptom. We have provided you with tools to help you in your efforts. Professionals and support groups can be there as your guides. Don't go it alone. Be patient, and learn to discover the ways in which you and the person you care about can enjoy one another and expand your relationship, even if the person is critically struggling with her eating and weight.

This is not an easy task. But if you continue in your efforts, there is much hope for the future.

We wish you good luck.

Notes

1. *New York Times,* sec. C, January 31, 1996.

2. "Psychological Treatment of Eating Disorders," *American Psychologist* 62, no. 3 (2007): 199–216.

3. L. L. Birch, K. K. Davison, and C. N. Markey, "A Longitudinal Examination of Patterns in Girls Weight Concerns and Body Dissatisfaction from Ages 5 to 9 Years," *International Journal of Eating Disorders* 33, no. 3 (2003): 320–32.

4. I. Cherney, M. Henninger, and A. Rudersdorf, "The Barbie Diet: Children's Perceptions of Body Image," presented at the meeting of the Midwestern Psychological Association, Chicago, 2007.

5. *Diagnostic and Statistical Manual of Mental Disorders,* 4th ed., text rev. (Arlington, VA: American Psychiatric Assocation, 2000).

6. Ibid.

7. Ibid.

8. Ibid.

9. Ibid.

10. C. Steiner-Adair, "The Body Politic: Normal Female Adolescent Development and the Development of Eating Disorders," *Journal of the American Academy of Psychoanalysis* 14 (1986): 95–114.

11. D. Mickley, "The Last Word," *Eating Disorders* 2, no. 2 (1994): 188–92.

12. K. Zerbe, *The Body Betrayed: A Deeper Understanding of Women, Eating Disorders, and Treatment* (Washington, DC: American Psychiatric Press, 1993).

13. *Pediatrics* 107, no. 1 (January 2001): 54–60.

14. D. Le Grange and J. Lock, *Family Based Treatment of Adolescent*

Anorexia Nervosa: The Maudsley Approach (Toronto: National Eating Disorder Information Centre, 2005).

15. I. Eisler, et al, "Family Therapy for Adolescent Anorexia Nervosa: The Results of a Controlled Comparison of Two Family Interventions," *Journal of Child Psychology and Psychiatry and Allied Disciplines* 41 (2000): 727–36.

16. B. Lask and R. Bryant-Waugh, *Childhood Onset Anorexia Nervosa and Related Eating Disorders* (East Sussex, UK: Psychology Press, 1993).

17. Mark A.Blais, et al., "Pregnancy: Outcome and Impact on Symptomatology in a Cohort of Eating-Disordered Women," *International Journal of Eating Disorders* 27, no. 1 (January 2000): 140–49.

18. R. J. Wurtman and J. J. Wurtman, "Brain Serotonin, Carbohydrate Craving, Obesity and Depression," *Obesity Research* 3 (1995): 477S–80S.

19. V. Vaido, "Cognitive Behavioral Therapy for Binge Eating Disorder," *Advanced Psychosomatic Medicine* 27 (2006): 86–93.

20. N. Berkman, K. Lohr, and C. Bulik. "Outcomes of Eating Disorders: A Systematic Review of the Literature," *International Journal of Eating Disorders* 40 (2007): 293–309.

21. L. K. Hsu et al., "Non-surgical Factors that Influence the Outcome of Bariatric Surgery: A Review," *Psychosomatic Medicine* 60 (1998): 338–46.

Resources

National Referral and Self-Help Organizations

The following organizations provide the names of therapists, doctors, outpatient facilities, and hospitals. We are providing these links to help you find out more about eating disorders and to help you find the best care.

Academy for Eating Disorders

www.aedweb.org
60 Revere Drive, Suite 500
Northbrook, IL 60062–1577
Telephone: (847) 498–4274
E-mail: info@aedweb.org

The Academy for Eating Disorders is an international professional organization that promotes excellence in research, treatment, and prevention of eating disorders. The AED provides education, training, and a forum for collaboration and professional dialogue.

Ackerman Institute for the Family

www.ackerman.org
149 East 78th Street
New York, NY 10021
Telephone: (212) 879–4900
E-mail: ackerman@ackerman.org

Ackerman Institute provides comprehensive family therapy. Ackerman's fees are on a sliding scale. Medicaid is accepted, and some managed care plans are honored.

Eating Disorder Referral and Information Center

www.edreferral.com

2923 Sandy Pointe, Suite 6

Del Mar, CA 92014–2052

Telephone: (858) 792–7463

E-mail: edreferral@aol.com

EDReferral.com has become well known for its dedication to the treatment and prevention of eating disorders. It has developed a reputation as the leading resource for those seeking referrals to eating disorders specialists. Each month's newsletter contains information on upcoming retreats, workshops, training, lectures, outreach, conferences, books, online support, treatment center news, support groups, and more.

Eating Disorder Resource Center

www.edrcnyc.org

330 West 58th Street, Suite 206

New York, NY 10019

Telephone: (212) 989–3987

E-mail: drjbris@yahoo.com

EDRC is one of the pioneering organizations in the field of eating disorders. Since 1980, EDRC has developed and offered specialized treatment programs for the eating-disordered population. The center provides a psychotherapy referral service in the New York/tri-state area that offers the most up-to-date, professional treatment available for problematic eating behaviors, food obsessions, and body image concerns. Dr. Judith Brisman is the director and cofounder of the center.

International Association of Eating Disorders Professionals

www.iaedp.com

P.O. Box 1295

Pekin, IL 61555–1295

Telephone: (800) 800–8126

E-mail: iaedpmembers@earthlink.net

The International Association of Eating Disorders Professionals is recognized for its excellence in providing first-quality education and high-level training standards to an international multidisciplinary group of health care providers and helping professions who treat the full spectrum of eating disorder problems.

My ED Help

www.myedhelp.com

My ED Help is a new online treatment finder and recovery network, disseminating information about eating disorders for both professionals and individuals concerned about their own health.

National Association of Anorexia Nervosa and Associated Disorders

www.anad.org

P.O. Box 7

Highland Park, IL 60035

Telephone: (847) 831–3438

E-mail: anadhelp@anad.org

ANAD was the first association in the United States developed for the education and support of individuals and families combating anorexia nervosa and bulimia. ANAD has listings of therapists and hospitals internationally. The association sponsors support groups throughout the country, conferences, advocacy campaigns, and research. In addition, it has a crisis hotline that operates from 9:00 a.m. to 5:00 p.m. Monday through Friday at the above number.

National Eating Disorders Association

www.nationaleatingdisorders.com

603 Stewart Street, Suite 803

Seattle, WA 98101

Telephone: (206) 382–3587

E-mail: info@NationalEatingDisorders.org

NEDA is dedicated to expanding public understanding of eating disorders and promoting access to quality treatment for those affected along with support for their families through education, advocacy, and research.

Somethingfishy: Web Site on Eating Disorders

www.something-fishy.org

Something Fishy is a Web site dedicated to raising awareness about eating disorders. Information is available about anorexia, bulimia, and compulsive overeating—definitions, signs and symptoms, physical dangers, online support, and so much more. Something Fishy emphasizes that eating disorders are not about food and weight; they are just the symptoms of something deeper going on inside. Something Fishy is determined to remind sufferers that they are not alone and that complete recovery is possible.

12-Step Self-Help Organizations

Alcoholics Anonymous

AA World Services, Inc.

www.aa.org

P.O. Box 459

New York, NY 10163

Telephone: (212) 870–3400

AA is a free 12-step self-help fellowship open to anyone concerned about a problem with alcohol. Twelve-step programs related to other concerns, such as drug abuse and gambling, are also available. Al-Anon and Children of Alcoholics are organizations for people whose lives have been affected by someone else's alcohol use. Check online for local organizations.

Overeaters Anonymous Headquarters

www.oa.org

P.O. Box 44020

Rio Rancho, NM 87174–4020

Telephone: (505) 891–2664

OA is a 12-step self-help fellowship of men and women who meet in order to help solve a common problem: compulsive overeating. Free local meetings are listed online. Inquire regarding specialized meetings for bulimics and anorexics.

Suggested Readings

Bloom, Carol, Andrea Gitter, Susan Gutwill, Laura Kogel, and Lela Zaphiropoulos. *Eating Problems: A Feminist Psychoanalytic Treatment Model.* New York: Basic Books, 1994.

Brown, Sheila. *What Do Mothers Want? Developmental Perspectives, Clinical Challenges.* New York: Analytic Press, 2005.

Bruch, Hilde. *Eating Disorders: Obesity, Anorexia and the Person Within.* New York: Basic Books, 1985.

Costin, Carolyn. *Your Dieting Daughter: Is She Dying for Attention?* New York: Bruner/Mazel, 1996.

Fairburn, C. G. *Cognitive Behavior Therapy and Eating Disorders.* New York: Guilford Press, 2008.

Fairburn, C. G. *Overcoming Binge Eating.* New York: Guilford Press, 1995.

Fairburn, C. G., and K. D. Brownell, eds. *Eating Disorders and Obesity: A Comprehensive Handbook* (2nd ed.). New York: Guilford Press, 2002.

Fish, Donna. *Take the Fight Out of Food: How to Prevent and Solve Your Child's Eating Problems.* New York: Atria Books, 2005.

Garner, David M., and Paul E. Garfinkel. *Handbook of Psychotherapy for Anorexia Nervosa and Bulimia.* New York: Guilford Press, 1997.

Hall, Lindsey. *Full Lives.* Carlsbad, CA: Gürze Books, 1993.

Hall, Lindsey, and Leigh Cohn. *Bulimia: A Guide to Recovery.* Carlsbad, CA: Gürze Books, 1999.

Herrin, Marcia, and Nancy Matsumoto. *The Parent's Guide to Eating Disorders: Supporting Self-Esteem, Healthy Eating, and Positive Body Image at Home.* Carlsbad, CA: Gürze Books, 2007.

Hirschmann, Jane, and Carol Munter. *When Women Stop Hating Their Bodies.* New York: Fawcett, 1995.

Johnson, Craig, ed. *Psychodynamic Treatment of Anorexia Nervosa and Bulimia.* New York: Guilford Press, 1991.

Lask, B., and R. Bryant-Waugh, eds. *Anorexia Nervosa and Related Disorders in Childhood and Adolescence* (2nd ed.). East Sussex, UK: Psychology Press, 2000.

Lock, James, and Daniel Le Grange. *Help Your Teenager Beat an Eating Disorder.* New York: Guilford Press, 2005.

Maine, Margo. *Father Hunger: Fathers, Daughters, and Food.* Carlsbad, CA: Gürze Books, 1991.

Munter, Carol, and Jane R. Hirschmann. *Overcoming Overeating.* Reading, MA: Addison-Wesley, 1988.

Orbach, Susie. *Fat Is a Feminist Issue II.* New York: Berkeley Trade, 1991.

Rabinor, Judith R. *A Starving Madness: Tales of Hunger, Hope and Healing in Psychotherapy.* Carlsbad, CA: Gürze Books, 2002.

Roth, Geneen. *Breaking Free from Compulsive Eating.* New York: Plume Books, 2003.

———. *When Food Is Love.* New York: Plume Books, 1991.

Stober, Michael, and Meg Schneider. *Just a Little Too Thin.* Cambridge, MA: Da Capo Press, 2006.

Treasure, J., G. Smith, and A. Crane. *Skills-based Learning for Caring for a Loved One with an Eating Disorder: The New Maudsley Method.* London and New York: Routledge, 2007.

Yalom, Irvin, and Joellen Werne. *Treating Eating Disorders.* San Francisco: Jossey-Bass, 1996.

Zerbe, Kathryn J. *The Body Betrayed: A Deeper Understanding of Women, Eating Disorders, and Treatment.* Washington, DC: American

Psychiatric Press, 1993.

————. *Integrated Treatment of Eating Disorders: Beyond the Body Betrayed.* New York: Norton, 2008.

Journals

Eating Disorders: The Journal of Treatment and Prevention (quarterly publication).

International Journal of Eating Disorders (quarterly publication).

Related Subjects

Alcoholism and Substance Abuse

AA World Services. *The Big Book.* New York, 2001.

————. *Living Sober.* New York, 2004.

Brown, Stephanie. *A Place Called Self: Women, Sobriety and Radical Transformation.* Chicago: Hazelden, 2004.

Kinney, Jean. *Loosening the Grip: A Handbook of Alcohol Information.* New York: McGraw-Hill, 2005.

Levin, Jerome D. *Alcoholism: A Bio-Psycho-Social Approach.* New York: Hemisphere, 1990.

Meyers, Robert J., and Brenda L. Wolfe. *Get Your Loved One Sober: Alternatives to Nagging, Pleading, and Threatening.* Chicago: Hazelden, 2003.

Vaillant, George E. *The Natural History of Alcoholism—Causes, Patterns, and Paths to Recovery.* Cambridge, MA: Harvard University Press, 1983.

Washton, Arnold M., and Donna Boundy. *Willpower's Not Enough: Understanding and Recovering from Addictions of Every Kind.* New York: HarperCollins, 1990.

Washton, Arnold M., and Joan E. Zweben. *Treating Alcohol and Drug Problems in Psychotherapy Practice*. New York: Guilford Press, 2006.

Children of Alcoholics

Black, Claudia. *It Will Never Happen to Me!* Denver: MAC Printing and Publications Division, 2001.

Conyers, B. *Addict in the Family: Stories of Loss, Hope, and Recovery.* Chicago: Hazelden, 2003.

Seixas, Judith S., and Geraldine Youcha. *Children of Alcoholism: A Survivor's Manual.* New York: Crown, 1986.

Incest

Bass, Ellen, and Laura Davis. *The Courage to Heal: A Guide for Women Survivors of Child Sexual Abuse*. New York: Collins, 2008.

Davies, Jodie Messier, and Mary Gail Frawley. *Treating the Adult Survivor of Childhood Sexual Abuse*. New York: Basic Books, 1994.

Change

Jordan, Judith, Alexandra Kaplan, Jean Baker Miller, Irene Stiver, and Janet Surrey. *Women's Growth in Connection: Writings from the Stone Center.* New York: Guilford Press, 1991.

Lerner, Harriet Goldhor. *The Dance of Anger: A Woman's Guide to Changing the Patterns of Intimate Relationships.* New York: Harper & Row, 1997.

Pipher, Mary. *Reviving Ophelia: Saving the Selves of Adolescent Girls.* New York: Putnam, 1994.

Parenting

Cohen-Sandler, Roni, and Michelle Silver. *"I'm Not Mad, I Just Hate You!" A New Understanding of Mother–Daughter Conflict: Surviving and Thriving during Your Daughter's Teenage Years.* New York: Penguin Putnam, 1999.

Mogel, Wendy. *The Blessing of a Skinned Knee: Using Jewish Teachings to Raise Self-Reliant Children.* New York: Penguin Compass, 2001.

Seigel, D., & M. Hartzell. *Parenting from the Inside Out: How a Deeper Self-Understanding Can Help You Raise Children Who Thrive.* New York: Archer/Putnam, 2003.

Taffel, Ron. *Getting through to Difficult Kids and Parents: Uncommon Sense for Child Professionals.* New York: Guilford Press, 2001.

Taffel, Ron, and Melinda Blau. *Parenting by Heart: How to Stay Connected to Your Child in a Disconnected World.* Cambridge, MA: Perseus Books, 2002.

Index